# HOMEMADE CANDY

*Other cookbooks by Farm Journal*

FARM JOURNAL'S COUNTRY COOKBOOK

FREEZING & CANNING COOKBOOK

FARM JOURNAL'S COMPLETE PIE COOKBOOK

LET'S START TO COOK

COOKING FOR COMPANY

HOMEMADE BREAD

AMERICA'S BEST VEGETABLE RECIPES

BY THE FOOD EDITORS OF FARM JOURNAL

# HOMEMADE CANDY

EDITED BY

NELL B. NICHOLS

*FARM JOURNAL* FIELD FOOD EDITOR

PHOTOGRAPHY SUPERVISED BY

AL J. REAGAN

*FARM JOURNAL* ART STAFF

DOUBLEDAY & COMPANY, INC.

GARDEN CITY, NEW YORK

Library of Congress Catalog Card Number 79–121953
Copyright © 1970 by Farm Journal, Inc.
Printed in the United States of America

# Contents

# CONFECTIONS

# COLOR ILLUSTRATIONS

# Everyone Likes Candy!

How long has it been since you've cut creamy-smooth squares of chocolate fudge to pass on a plate to guests? When did you last stretch a batch of amber peanut brittle out thin on a marble slab, then crack it into bite-size chunks? Have you ever lined a gift box with lacy paper doilies and filled it with your own hand-dipped chocolates, each piece monogrammed with a dribble of chocolate to tell what the center is—N for nougat, V for vanilla cream, X for caramel?

Do your children or grandchildren know what an old-fashioned taffy pull is? Or how to *make* marshmallows? Would you like to beat the budget by making your own candy bars? (Imagine what good sellers they'll be at your next bazaar or carnival!)

Few treats from your kitchen bring as much happiness to family and friends as homemade candy. Almost every homemaker has a few treasured recipes, but the surprise of a new confection builds popularity as nothing else can.

And this cookbook has a wonderful collection of choice recipes—old favorites improved and retested to guarantee you good results. Plus scores of recipes for candies you may never have tried to make at home—Almond Paste, for instance, or Texas Pralines, Dipped Pretzels, Party Mints, Lollypops, Caramel Apples, shiny Glazed Almonds.

With the approach of Christmas, when you "deck your halls with holly" and decide on the most prominent spot for your tinseled tree, candy also moves to stage center—indeed, it becomes a kitchen campaign! The candy treats you make before the holidays are a friendly greeting to relatives and neighbors who stop by to nibble while they talk. Homemade candy also is something special to share with people far away. Packages holding coffee cans, stuffed with love and candy, travel from home kitchens to servicemen and students around the earth.

Although more people make more candy at Christmas time than all the rest of the year, candy is part of every festive celebration:

Easter, Valentine's Day, birthdays and parties of all kinds. People universally like candy! They may have to learn to like other foods, but the fondness for sweets comes naturally.

Like flowers, candy "speaks" eloquently; a box of homemade confections carries an especially thoughtful thank-you to your recent hostess. Little boys and girls deliver candy proudly to their grandparents and teachers—especially if they had a hand in making it. A batch of candy foresightedly stored in your freezer will be ready anytime to welcome young people returning home from school or work.

So many cherished memories come crowding back when you think about candy making. "My mother used to make this candy for us to eat on Christmas Eve while we decorated the tree," writes the contributor of Maple Penuche (see Index for recipe). And of course, she makes it now for her own family. Another woman sends the note, "Caramels are what Grandpa liked best for his birthday. So I always think of him when I make them." (Our recipe for Caramels Supreme [see Index for recipe] can be dipped in chocolate or not, as you prefer. Delicious either way!)

Homemade candy cheers the lonely, or sweetly says "I miss you." One woman writes: "I got one of our favorite candy recipes from an older woman who visited us for two weeks. She borrowed my kitchen to make a batch to mail to her husband back home—just to let him know she was thinking of him." (One of the candies we recommend for mailing is American-Style Nougat—it's a good keeper. See Index for recipe.)

Another candy maker says: "I'll never forget the knock on the door that afternoon one December 24 when we were almost feeling sorry for ourselves in a new home far away from relatives and friends. Nor will I forget the young man to whom we opened the door. He carried a box of candy; it was wrapped in white, tied with red ribbons and decorated with a few sprigs of evergreen. He said he and his mother lived on an adjoining farm and that they wanted to welcome us to our new home and wish us a Merry Christmas. Later my mother got the candy recipe from his mother. I've been making that candy year after year at Christmas time for that young man, now my husband." (Fudge earns a warm welcome wherever you take it. A recipe we're partial to is Burnt Sugar Fudge—it's different. See Index for recipe.)

Homemade candy at bazaars is always a money-maker par

excellence. "I took peanut brittle to a church food sale," one recipe contributor wrote. "It disappeared so fast that the women of the church adopted it as a money-making project. Every year they set aside time to make pounds and pounds of the brittle. They sell it at a good price—a needed boost for their budget." (If you use a candy thermometer as directed in our recipe for Salted Peanut Brittle de luxe, you'll insure success every time.)

Candy making draws the family together. "My husband helps me make divinity and popcorn balls every Christmas," confides a wife. "He beats the egg whites for divinity and pours the hot syrup when I take over beating the candy. Then he helps me spoon out the pieces onto waxed paper—that has to be done fast, before it sets. He pops corn while I cook the syrup. I shape the balls and he wraps them in plastic film and piles them in a miniature bushel basket that we put under the Christmas tree so our company can help themselves. There's always a race against time at our house and a helper speeds up the work." Another candy maker also enjoys working with her husband. She says: "It's more fun to make candy when you have a helper even though you have to watch him—he's tempted to sample too much while he works."

Half the pleasure of the old-time taffy pull was the talk and laughter. The fun built a bridge across the generations that today's parents might well envy. A FARM JOURNAL friend sent us this account of her remembrances: "Our taffy pulls usually were impromptu affairs. Everyone from Grandpa and Grandma to toddlers just had to stick his fingers into the candy. The pulling furnished the entertainment; the candy, the refreshments. I remember the spirit of togetherness between the generations. We're reviving the taffy pull for our children with considerable success."

While we'll not describe here all the new kinds of candy in this book, we must tell you about our homemade candy bars. Easy to make and eat, they're wonderful to snack on, to tuck into lunchboxes and to snag buyers at food sales. Be sure to look up the recipes. You'll want to try some first cousins of candy, too—our recipes for confections. No candy cookbook would be complete without them.

**The Magic of Sugar Cookery**   Candy making is sugar cookery. Learn how to handle sugar and liquid over heat, and you'll be a blue ribbon candy maker. The key is temperature, as you'll discover in the pages that follow. Sugar mixtures change character as they increase in temperature. An experiment will illustrate this.

Suppose you put sugar and water in a saucepan over heat, stirring the mixture until the sugar dissolves. Bring it to boiling and continue cooking it at a low boil until the syrup reaches the soft ball stage (232 to 240°). If you take some out at this point, you can make fondant with it.

If you continue cooking the syrup remaining in the saucepan until it reaches the firm ball stage (242 to 248°), you could remove a part of it to make caramels.

By cooking the rest of the syrup to the hard ball stage (250 to 268°), you could pour some out to cool and pull for taffy.

Continue cooking the syrup still in the saucepan to the soft crack stage (270 to 290°), and again pour out a part—you've got butterscotch.

Bring the last of the syrup to the hard crack stage (300 to 310°), and make lollypops for the children.

This is the magic of sugar syrup and temperature differences. With the same ingredients, you can make five kinds of candy! Of course, you add other ingredients to the candy—flavorings, nuts, chocolate, butter, coconut—to make it taste better and to get variety. Often, you add food color to step up eye appeal. But temperature remains the key to the kind of candy you make whenever you cook up a sugar mixture.

The recipes in this cookbook give the temperature to which you cook the candy, and we recommend that you use a good candy thermometer. In addition, we suggest that you do what we do in our own Test Kitchens: Make the cold water test, too. It's a double check to insure good results. You should test your thermometer before you use it to determine its accuracy at the elevation where you live; altitude makes a difference. You'll find simple directions for doing this in our book.

A change in atmospheric pressure on the day you make candy may make a difference, too. Perhaps you've noticed how experienced candy makers consider weather signs when they want to cook candy. They speak of "good candy weather." A fair, dry, cool day is ideal. If you want to make candy when it's raining or when wet snow is falling, you'll need to cook it to a couple of degrees higher temperature. Better still, retest your thermometer in boiling water on humid days, to get a reading for that day—directions are in this book.

Techniques also affect your candy results. In this book we explain them—what to do and what to avoid doing. Also we share many clever tricks candy makers have discovered to produce more attractive and better candy, to cut down costs and simplify the work involved.

You will notice that the traditional tried-and-true recipes in this cookbook are updated to use ingredients, methods and appliances available today, such as the electric mixer. You also will find that new versions of old-time favorites are equally as tasty, even though they use some surprise ingredients. Fudge is an example—you might find marshmallow creme or evaporated milk listed in the recipe ingredients. Corn syrup, an enemy of grainy, sugary candy, plays an important role in contemporary candy making. Many of the new recipes yield larger amounts of candy—4 to 5½ pounds. You used to make two or three batches to get this much. "My husband," one woman confesses, "always complained that the fudge plate seemed never to get around twice at holiday time." Try our larger recipes if you hear this at your house!

No matter which of our tempters you try first, we guarantee pleasing results (if you follow directions, of course), enjoyment —and compliments.

# CANDIES

# How to Make Perfect Candy

Do exactly as your recipe directs when you're ready to cook candy. We list here some of the basic rules, but remember that there are variations to all rules. If the recipe you're using gives different directions, follow *your* recipe.

Use a fairly deep, large, thick or heavy saucepan with straight sides.

When you put the candy on to cook, stir it until the sugar dissolves and comes to a boil; then stir only enough to prevent sticking to the pan and scorching. Use a wooden spoon or your paddle-type candy thermometer. Rinse and dry spoon before you use it to make cold water tests or to beat candy after cooking. This is a safeguard against grainy candy.

Cook candy at a fairly low, but steady boil. *Steady* is the important word.

When the candy mixture comes to a boil, remove any sugar crystals that form on the side of the saucepan. Do this throughout the cooking if necessary. To remove crystals, wrap a strip of cheesecloth or other clean cloth around the tines of a table fork. Dip in cold water, squeeze out the excess water and wipe off the crystals. Rinse crystals off the cloth and squeeze, so you'll be ready to wipe off other crystals if they form. Or dip a pastry brush in cold water and use it instead of the cloth-covered fork. Rinse sugar crystals off the brush after use, too.

Many candy cooks cover the saucepan for 3 minutes when the candy mixture comes to a boil. The steam dissolves crystals that form. Watch carefully that the syrup doesn't boil over. Put the candy thermometer into saucepan when you uncover candy. If crystals appear later, wipe them off with a damp cloth-covered fork or pastry brush.

When the candy is cooked (see tests below), remove the thermometer at once, or large sugar crystals may form around it and make the candy grainy. When the recipe directs you to cool the cooked candy, without stirring, to lukewarm, before you begin to beat it, be sure to cool it to lukewarm. Recipes often give the luke-warm temperature (110°), but don't worry about having removed the thermometer; it's easy to judge the temperature by feeling the bottom of the pan with your hand. It should feel neither warm nor cool. The candy will be grainy if not cooled enough; *sugar crystals form readily when you stir or beat warm candy*. It's better to have the candy mixture on the cool side rather than warmer than lukewarm. The cooler the candy, the more difficult it is to beat—but the creamier it will be.

Once you start the beating, keep at it until it is ready to pour or drop from a spoon. You need not beat it fast, but steadily. You can successfully use a combination of stirring and beating.

To pour candy into a pan to cool, bring the saucepan holding the hot mixture down close to the pan. Pour quickly and do not scrape out the remnants that stick to the saucepan. They may contain a few large sugar crystals—enough to spoil the entire batch. (Even one large crystal encourages other crystals to form and gather round. That's the way rock candy is made.)

*Lightly* butter, grease or oil pan before you pour the candy into it to cool. A heavy coating makes the candy greasy and less pleasant to eat from the hand.

If you aren't going to serve the candy shortly after it is set or firm, keep it in a cool place. In case you wish to keep it several weeks or longer, layer it between pieces of waxed paper in a container and cover tightly. Store in the freezer.

## HOW TO TELL WHEN CANDY IS COOKED

Cooking candy to the correct temperature is critical to success. There are two ways to find out when it is cooked enough—making the cold water test and reading the temperature with a good candy thermometer. FARM JOURNAL food editors make both tests and recommend that you do the same. You'll get a double check.

**Cold Water Test** Remove saucepan of cooking candy from heat when thermometer in it registers at least 2° below the temperature specified in recipe. If you leave it on the heat until temperature is reached, it can quickly overcook. Drop no more than ½ tsp. of hot syrup from spoon into very cold (but not ice) water. Let stand 1

minute. Pick it up with your fingers so you can feel the stage to
which candy has cooked.

*Soft Ball:* Hot syrup makes a soft ball when you pick it up, but it
does not hold its shape (232 to 240°). For fudge, penuche and
fondant.

*Firm Ball:* Hot syrup makes a firm ball that holds its shape when
you pick it up (242 to 248°). For caramels and caramel corn.

*Hard Ball:* Syrup makes a hard ball. It feels hard when you
pick it up, but is still plastic (250 to 268°). For divinity and taffy.

*Soft Crack:* Syrup forms hard, but not brittle threads rather than
a ball (270 to 290°). For toffee and butterscotch.

*Hard Crack:* Syrup forms brittle threads that break between
your fingers (300 to 310°). For brittles, lollypops and caramel or
candy apples.

**How to Use Your Candy Thermometer** Check the accuracy of
your thermometer. Place it in a saucepan of vigorously boiling
water for a few minutes. Then read the temperature without removing thermometer. It should be at 212° if your thermometer is
accurate and you live at sea level. (Water boils at 212° at sea
level, at lower temperatures in higher elevations. Subtract 1° for
every 500 feet above sea level.) If water boils when thermometer
registers 210°, it registers 2° low. This means your candy is done
2° lower than your recipe calls for. If water boils at 214° on your
thermometer, add 2° to the temperature specified in recipe. Check-
ing your thermometer enables you to correct differences due to the
inaccuracy of your thermometer and/or altitude.

Many expert candy makers check their thermometers every time
they make candy, for this also corrects variations due to weather.
If you do not check your thermometer on rainy, humid days, cook
the candy 1 or 2° higher than on less humid, fair days. Or cook it
to a slightly firmer stage when tested in cold water.

You can put the thermometer in candy mixture before you start
cooking it or when it comes to a boil. (If you cover saucepan
when syrup reaches a boil and let mixture boil 3 minutes as a
safeguard against sugar crystals forming, put the thermometer in
when you remove the saucepan cover.)

Make sure that the boiling syrup completely covers the thermometer bulb and that the bulb does not rest on the bottom of

the pan. A paddle-type candy thermometer with 2° graduations is an excellent investment.

Watch temperature closely after it reaches 220°. It rises fast after this point.

Read the thermometer at eye level. Hold it in hot candy in vertical position near the front of the saucepan. If it is difficult to see the graduations, use a magnifying glass.

When the temperature reaches the temperature given in recipe, the candy is cooked. Remove thermometer at once or large sugar crystals may form around it and make the candy grainy.

Let the thermometer cool before you wash it, to avoid breakage.

# Major Ingredients in Candy Making

Sugar is the heroine of the candy story. The way it behaves in the saucepan largely determines the quality of the candy. The first step is to use the kind of sugar specified in your recipe. Here are the types called for in this cookbook:

*Granulated:* This is fully refined sugar, in the form of small white grains. Take your pick of sugars made from sugar cane or sugar beets. You can use them interchangeably. When a recipe simply calls for "sugar" without a description, use this white sugar. Store it in tightly covered containers once you bring a supply to your kitchen. This will keep the moisture out. One pound measures 2¼ to 2½ cups.

*Superfine:* As its name indicates, this is an exceedingly fine granulated sugar. It dissolves so quickly it's sometimes called "instant" sugar. If your recipe calls for it and you do not have a supply in your cupboard, you can substitute regular granulated sugar. One pound of superfine sugar measures 2⅓ cups.

*Confectioners':* Many people west of the Mississippi River call it powdered sugar. It is granulated sugar that has been ground into a powder, soft and fluffy. It contains a tiny amount of cornstarch to prevent excessive lumping. Store it like granulated sugar in a tightly covered container. One pound, unsifted, measures 4 cups; sifted, 1 pound measures 4½ to 5 cups.

*Brown:* All brown sugars, light to dark, are "soft" sugars, with a very small crystal size, which gives them their soft, spongy texture. The intensity of color and pleasing flavor comes from the amount of molasses syrup which clings to the crystals . . . the darker the sugar, the stronger the flavor. Store all brown sugars in airtight containers to retain the natural moisture. You can transfer sugar from package to wide-mouthed glass jars with tight lids and store in cupboard or refrigerator. Or you can pack it into plastic bags, close them tightly and put them in the refrigerator. Some brown sugar comes to markets in these bags. If brown sugar begins to get lumpy and hard, you can redeem it; spread it in a shallow pan and heat in a very low oven until it softens. Then use it promptly, for after cooling it gets harder than before. In this cookbook, unless otherwise stated, our recipes were tested with light brown sugar. One pound of light brown sugar, firmly packed, measures about 2⅓ cups; 1 pound of dark brown sugar, firmly packed, measures 2⅛ to 2¼ cups.

*Colored Sugars:* These sugar crystals come in a wide variety of attractive colors. You find them at your supermarket in tiny jars or see-through bags. Sprinkle them on candies for pleasing garnishes.

*Cubes or Tablets:* Because these sugars are a charming sweetening for hot tea, this cookbook gives directions for decorating them with tinted frostings in dainty designs. They add a pretty note to tea parties and, boxed with a frill of paper doily, they make delightful gifts.

*Special Sugars:* There are special sugars, but they are not available everywhere. Granulated brown sugar is one of these. It is free flowing. Frosting sugar, available mainly in the West, dissolves instantly and never requires sifting. The particles of confectioners' (powdered) sugar are processed so that they hold together in tiny balls, like popped corn in popcorn balls. It contains no cornstarch.

## SYRUPS PLAY SUPPORTING ROLES

In the theater everyone tiptoes around the temperamental star, trying to humor her and save the show. If you think of sugar as the star in candy making, the syrups must be called the supporting players—they do such a lot to make the star look good! Give syrups credit for the marvelous creamy smoothness of fudge, divinity and penuche. Here's how sugar and syrup work together:

The big challenge every candy maker faces is how to keep the sugar crystals so small that no one notices them. Even the smoothest fudge or fondant, for instance, has tiny sugar crystals, but because they are so small, you think the candy is creamy and smooth as satin.

It's natural for sugar, combined with a liquid like milk or water, to be grainy or sugary after cooking. Sugar is sucrose, which dries out and recrystallizes. Corn syrup, on the other hand, is largely what home economists call dextrose and levulose, or invert sugars. Instead of drying out, candies that contain sufficient amounts of invert sugars absorb moisture from the air and do not recrystallize.

Also, during cooking, they invert some of the sucrose (granulated sugar). What corn syrup does is help prevent the formation of large sugar crystals.

Other food substances, such as lemon juice, cream of tartar and vinegar also help keep candy from becoming sugary, but they're not so dependable as corn syrup. Grandmother had science on her side when she added vinegar to white taffy and made molasses taffy.

Here are some of the most widely distributed syrups for candies:

*Cane:* It comes in dark and light colors and is made from sugar cane.

*Corn:* Made from corn, this syrup can be either light or dark. The light syrup is bleached and clarified in processing; the dark is blended with refiners' syrup left after refining raw sugar. In our recipes we specify whether to use light or dark corn syrup. When you pour this syrup from the bottle, wipe the neck and recap the bottle tightly before putting it away in the cupboard. This makes the bottle easier to open the next time and helps to prevent mold and crystallization.

*Honey:* The bees make honey from the nectar they gather from flowers; the flavor depends on the blossoms or fields they visit. There is more clover and alfalfa honey on the market than other kinds and jars are almost always labeled. Light color indicates a mild flavor. Strained honey, the kind used in candy making, is extracted from the honeycomb, strained and clarified. Keep honey tightly covered in a dry place. Chilling makes it cloudy. If it becomes sugary, set the open container of honey in a saucepan containing lukewarm water and heat until it becomes syrupy. The world's first candies and confections were sweetened with honey.

*Maple:* If your maple syrup is labeled 100 per cent, it is the boiled-down sap of maple trees. Since it takes so much sap to make a quart of this syrup, it is rather expensive. More widely available are maple sugar syrup (maple sugar with water added) and maple-blended syrup (a mixture of other syrups with some syrup made from maple sugar). Once you open the container of maple syrup of any kind, keep it covered in the refrigerator to discourage mold from forming. If mold appears, skim it off and heat the syrup to a boil, cool and refrigerate.

*Molasses:* This sweetener is processed from the concentrated juice of sugar cane. You can buy light or unsulphured molasses and a darker, sulphured molasses with stronger flavor, which results when sulphur fumes are used in the sugar refining process. Recipes in this cookbook specify when to use light or dark molasses. (Nutrition conscious candy makers never forget that molasses is a rich source of food iron.)

## OTHER INGREDIENTS FOR CANDY MAKING

When Christmas is in the air, many women look in their cupboards and refrigerators to take stock of ingredients they'll need to make holiday candy. Here are some of the foods the candy recipes in this cookbook call for:

**Butter or Margarine**    Many candy cooks prefer the flavor of butter, but both margarine and butter contribute the desired richness. If you use margarine, either the regular or soft kind is satisfactory, although soft margarine contains less fat.

**Cream:** Recipes call for both heavy (whipping) and light cream. Whipping cream is available nationally, but in many localities light cream is not. You can substitute dairy half-and-half for it, but it contains less butter fat (10 to 12 per cent). Light cream has no less than 18 per cent butter fat. You can duplicate light cream by combining equal parts of heavy cream and 3 per cent whole milk. Dairy sour cream lends its delightful flavor to some candies and confections.

**Canned Milk:** Evaporated and sweetened condensed milk contribute frequently to the goodness and smoothness of candies. They are two entirely different products, and are not interchangeable. Be sure you use the one the recipe lists.

**Dry Milk:** This adds extra protein to some candies.

**Flavorings and Extracts:** While vanilla is the basic and favorite flavoring, there are many other exciting kinds that add variety in taste. It pays to buy well-known, quality brands. For economy, buy a large or medium bottle of vanilla extract instead of a small one. Keep the bottle tightly closed and as far away from oven heat as the size of your kitchen permits. Some of the other flavorings called for in this cookbook are almond, lemon, orange, pistachio, black walnut, maple and peppermint extracts. Oil of peppermint, spearmint, wintergreen, lemon, orange and anise also are ingredients in some recipes. These flavorings, which you buy at drugstores, are so strong that you use only a few drops. When buying them, tell the druggist you will use the oil to flavor food.

**Chocolate:** Unsweetened chocolate squares, semisweet chips and squares, sweet cooking chocolate, milk chocolate and cocoa are all important in candy making. Also see Dipping Chocolates in Index for the different kinds of confection coatings for candies.

**Food Colors:** The two types are liquid and paste colors. Both are certified by the Food and Drug Administration as safe. They come in a wide array of colors and you can mix them to make all the tints in between. You'll find liquid colors in practically all supermarkets. Some candy makers greatly prefer paste food colors, especially for hard candies; they contain no water. But either kind may be used with good results.

**Coconut:** Use the kind specified—the flaked, shredded or finely grated cookie coconut.

**Gelatin:** Both unflavored and fruit flavored gelatins are important in candy making.

**Fruits:** Dried dates, apricots, raisins, prunes, figs and applesauce are the basis for excellent confections. Orange and lemon juice and grated peel also enhance the taste of candy.

**Nuts:** Adding different kinds of nuts to candies and confections is one of the most enjoyable ways of providing flavor changes along with interesting texture. Among the kinds featured in our candy recipes are almonds, black walnuts, Brazil nuts, cashews, filberts, peanuts, pistachio nuts, pecans, walnuts and mixed nuts. Hickory nuts and butternuts are available in some country kitchens and many of the recipes sent by Oregon and California women call for walnuts. They explain that walnut trees grow near their ranch homes, often in their yards. Southern homemakers contribute recipes rich and luscious with their native pecans. Black walnut trees grow in a wide area and their fruit still holds the affection of many farm candy makers.

If you shell your nuts, keep the kernels in covered containers or tightly closed plastic bags. Put them in the freezer or refrigerator. If you buy shelled nuts in plastic bags, cans or glass jars, also keep them, after opening, in the freezer or refrigerator. Use unsalted nuts unless recipe specifies the salted kind.

**Marshmallows and Marshmallow Creme:** Both regular size and miniature marshmallows contribute smoothness and flavor to candies. Once you open the package rewrap them and keep them in the freezer. Marshmallow creme is an important ingredient in the newer type fudges.

**Popcorn:** Some time when you're in a supermarket, take stock of the many kinds of popcorn confections. You may be surprised how numerous they are. And look at the collection of recipes for similar snacks in this cookbook. Many women fix them in their country kitchens. Just reading the recipes will make you downright hungry and eager to start cooking some wonderful treats.

# Equipment for Candy Making

Heavy Saucepans with straight sides in 2-qt., 3-qt. and 4-qt. or larger sizes. Deep saucepans are desirable because liquid evaporates too fast in shallow pans.

Double Boiler in 1½-qt., 2-qt. or 3-qt. sizes

Candy Thermometer of the paddle type with 2° graduations

Food Chopper (Grinder)

Pastry Brush

Electric Mixer or Beater

Household Scales (optional)

Wooden Spoons with long handles

Broad Spatula with steel blade that does not bend easily

Pans for cooling candy: 13×9×2″, 8 and 9″ square, 15½× 10½×1″ (jelly roll), 9×5×3″ and 8×4×2½″ (loaf pans) and baking sheets or large platters

Strainer

Grater

Kitchen Scissors

Wire Cake Racks

Knives for cutting candy and chopping nuts

Measuring Cups

Measuring Spoons

Bowls of various sizes

Wooden Skewers for lollypops and caramel or candy apples

Marble Slab or Plastic Kitchen Counter Top

Cast Iron (heavy) Skillet in 9 or 10″ sizes

Airtight Containers for storing candy

NOTE: Along with the equipment listed above, you will need waxed paper, and aluminum foil or plastic wrap.

# Memorable Traditional Fudge

When you hear someone speak longingly of "the wonderful fudge that Mamma used to make," you may be sure that Mamma had a good recipe—and a sure touch—for making classic fudge. This unforgettable fudge is the kind made with sugar, unsweetened chocolate, milk, butter, corn syrup, vanilla and nuts harvested on the farm.

It's difficult to imagine any more superior homemade candy than our Chocolate Fudge Velvet, Black Walnut/Chocolate Fudge or Blond Fudge Supreme. Our recipes for them are classics updated; if you're an inexperienced candy maker, follow these modernized directions, which eliminate guesswork, and you'll have good luck.

Avoid the two most common mistakes—beating the cooked candy *too soon* and *too little*. If you beat it before it cools to lukewarm, you can depend on grainy or sugary fudge. And if you stop beating it too soon, the candy will lack that marvelous creaminess for which fudge is famed. Beat it until a small amount dropped from a spoon holds its shape. Then pour it into the pan at once. If it balks on spreading evenly, just knead it gently a few times with your fingers until you can manipulate it. Even if it isn't satiny smooth on top, it will be creamy and delicious.

## CHOCOLATE FUDGE VELVET

*Creamy, luscious, smooth-as-velvet, classic fudge—sweet perfection*

3 squares unsweetened chocolate, cut in pieces
1 c. milk
3 c. sugar
3 tblsp. light corn syrup

⅛ tsp. salt
3 tblsp. butter or margarine
1½ tsp. vanilla
½ c. chopped walnuts or pecans (optional)

Combine chocolate and milk in 3-qt. heavy saucepan. Cook over low heat, stirring constantly, until milk is scalded and chocolate is melted. Stir in sugar, corn syrup and salt.

Cook over medium heat, stirring until sugar dissolves. If sugar crystals form on sides of pan, wipe them off.

Cook without stirring until mixture reaches the soft ball stage (236 to 238°).

Remove from heat; add butter without stirring. Let stand without disturbing until mixture cools to lukewarm (110°).

Add vanilla. Beat until candy loses its gloss and starts to thicken. Stir in nuts and pour quickly into a lightly buttered 8″ square pan. (Do not scrape pan.) Mark in 36 pieces while still warm; when cold and firm, cut. Makes about 1½ pounds.

NOTE: You can substitute ½ c. cocoa for the chocolate. Add it to the sugar and salt (in saucepan) and mix thoroughly. Then add milk and corn syrup and cook as for Chocolate Fudge Velvet. Increase butter or margarine from 3 tblsp. to ⅓ c.

## KNEADED CHOCOLATE FUDGE

*Ideal candy for mailing—pack unsliced rolls in cans or mailing tubes*

| | |
|---|---|
| 2 squares unsweetened chocolate, cut in pieces | ⅛ tsp. salt |
| | 1 tsp. vinegar |
| 1 c. milk | 2 tblsp. butter or margarine |
| 3 c. sugar | 1 tsp. vanilla |
| ¼ c. light corn syrup | ½ c. chopped nuts |

Combine chocolate and milk in 3-qt. heavy saucepan. Cook over low heat, stirring constantly, until milk is scalded and chocolate is melted. Stir in sugar, corn syrup and salt.

Place over medium heat and stir until sugar dissolves. If sugar crystals form on sides of pan, wipe them off. Cook at a steady, fairly low boil without stirring to the soft ball stage (238°). Remove from heat. Very gently stir in vinegar. Add butter without stirring. Cool until lukewarm (110°).

Add vanilla and beat until candy loses its gloss and starts to thicken. Stir in nuts.

Pour into lightly buttered pan or large platter. Let stand until cool enough to knead. Knead with fingers about 5 minutes.

Shape into 2 rolls, each about 2″ in diameter and about 5″ long. Wrap in waxed paper or foil and store in refrigerator or other cool place until ready to use. Slice slightly on diagonal in ½″ slices, wiping knife during cutting if fudge sticks to its blade. Makes 20 to 22 slices, or about 2 pounds.

**Candy Christmas Trees** From an Iowa farm kitchen comes this suggestion: Knead fudge and mold in lightly oiled or buttered Christmas tree gelatin salad molds (3½" long and 3" wide in broadest part is a good size). Cool and unmold. With a little encouragement from a knife at the base, the "trees" slip out easily. Decorate simply with white or tinted Ornamental Icing (see Index). Include at least one "fudge tree" in each gift box and one in the center of a plate of candy to promote conversation and compliments.

## Extra-Good Black Walnut Fudge

No reward for gathering, cracking and "picking out" black walnuts appeals more than a chance to help yourself to homemade candy in which the nuts star, according to a Kansas rancher on whose place several walnut trees grow along the creek. He rates Black Walnut/Chocolate Fudge one of the joys of country eating.

"Every year, as Christmas approaches," his daughter says, "Mother and I add our black walnuts to the fudge we make. This candy is our special gift to my aunts and uncles in Kansas City, who tell us the walnuts from the home ranch have an especially fresh taste lacking in nuts they buy in city shops. Maybe it's their imagination, but we all think the candy is exceptionally good."

### BLACK WALNUT/CHOCOLATE FUDGE

*Black walnuts and chocolate go together like peaches and cream*

2 squares unsweetened chocolate,
   cut in pieces
¾ c. milk
1 tblsp. light corn syrup
2 c. sugar

⅛ tsp. salt
2 tblsp. butter or margarine
1 tsp. vanilla
1 c. coarsely chopped black
   walnuts

Combine chocolate and milk in 2-qt. heavy saucepan. Cook over low heat, stirring constantly, until milk is scalded and chocolate is melted. Stir in corn syrup, sugar and salt.

Place over medium heat and stir until sugar is dissolved. If sugar crystals form on sides of pan, wipe them off. Cook without stirring at a fairly low boil to the soft ball stage (236°). Remove from heat. Add butter without stirring; cool to lukewarm (110°).

Add vanilla. Beat until candy loses its gloss and begins to thicken. Quickly stir in walnuts. Turn at once into a lightly buttered 8″ square pan. While warm, mark in 18 pieces.

When cool and firm, cut. Makes 1½ pounds.

N O T E : If black walnuts are not available, use chopped walnuts and add a few drops black walnut extract along with the vanilla.

## HONEYED FUDGE

*Honey imparts that good, old-time country flavor to chocolate fudge*

| | |
|---|---|
| 1 c. white sugar | ⅛ tsp. baking soda |
| 1 c. brown sugar | ¼ c. honey |
| ½ c. evaporated milk or light cream | 2 tblsp. butter or margarine |
| | ½ c. chopped nuts |
| ⅛ tsp. salt | ½ c. cookie coconut |
| 1 square unsweetened chocolate, broken in pieces | |

Combine white and brown sugars, evaporated milk, salt and chocolate in 2-qt. heavy saucepan. Cook slowly 5 minutes, stirring to dissolve sugars. If sugar crystals form on sides of pan, wipe them off. Add baking soda and honey. Continue cooking at a fairly low boil, stirring to prevent scorching, until mixture reaches the soft ball stage (238°). Remove from heat.

Add butter without stirring; cool to lukewarm (110°). Add nuts and coconut and beat vigorously until a little of candy dropped from spoon forms flat cakes. Pour into lightly buttered 8″ square pan; cool until firm. Cut in 36 pieces. Makes about 1½ pounds.

## PEANUT BUTTER FUDGE

*Peanut butter fans vote for this creamy chocolate candy*

| | |
|---|---|
| 3 c. sugar | 2 tblsp. light corn syrup |
| ¼ tsp. salt | 1 tsp. vanilla |
| 3 squares unsweetened chocolate | ¼ c. peanut butter |
| 1 c. milk | 1 c. coarsely broken nuts |

Combine sugar, salt, chocolate, milk and corn syrup in 3-qt heavy saucepan. Boil over medium heat, stirring until sugar dissolves. If sugar crystals form on sides of pan, wipe them off Cook until mixture reaches soft ball stage (234°).

Remove from heat; do not stir. Let cool until the bottom of the pan feels lukewarm to touch (110°).

Add vanilla and peanut butter and beat steadily until candy begins to lose its shine. Add nuts and pour quickly into buttered 8″ square pan. Cover and chill until firm. Cut into squares. Makes 36 squares or about 1½ pounds.

*Slick Trick:* Save the disposable foil pans which come with frozen and refrigerated foods from the supermarket. If you cool candy in these throwaway pans, you can cut it in neat, even pieces this way. Cut the corners of the pan, turn down the sides and slip the candy out in a block onto a cutting board. You won't have to dig into a pan to pry out the pieces.

## CHOCOLATE CHIP/PEANUT FUDGE

*If you like cookies with chocolate pieces, you'll like this candy*

2 c. sugar
⅔ c. milk
1 tblsp. butter or margarine
1 tsp. vanilla

3 tblsp. peanut butter
½ (6 oz.) pkg. chocolate chips
  (½ c.)

Combine sugar and milk in 2-qt. heavy saucepan; bring to a boil, stirring constantly, until sugar is dissolved. If sugar crystals form on sides of pan, wipe them off. Continue boiling without stirring to the soft ball stage (236°). Remove from heat.

Add butter without stirring; cool to lukewarm (110°).

Add vanilla and peanut butter; beat until mixture begins to thicken and lose its gloss. Stir in chocolate pieces at once and turn into slightly buttered 8½ × 4½ × 2½″ loaf pan. While warm, mark in 21 pieces. Cool until firm, then cut. Makes about 1 pound.

# Distinctive Banana/Chocolate Fudge

If you salvage fully ripe bananas in your freezer to use later in banana bread, here's another sweet use for the fruit. It's a good idea to put the peeled bananas through a food mill, although you can mash them thoroughly, add a little ascorbic acid powder to prevent discoloration, put in airtight containers in measured amounts, label and freeze. Then the bananas are measured and ready to go.

Of course you can make this moist, creamy Banana/Chocolate Fudge with fresh ripe bananas, thoroughly mashed.

## BANANA/CHOCOLATE FUDGE

*Brown sugar, chocolate, vanilla and bananas mingle flavors*

2 squares unsweetened chocolate, cut in pieces
½ c. brown sugar
1½ c. white sugar
1 medium ripe banana, mashed (⅓ c.)
¾ c. milk
⅛ tsp. salt
2 tblsp. light corn syrup
3 tblsp. butter or margarine
½ tsp. vanilla
½ c. chopped walnuts (optional)

Combine chocolate, brown and white sugars, banana, milk, salt and corn syrup. Cook over medium heat, stirring constantly, until sugars dissolve. If sugar crystals form on sides of pan, wipe them off. Continue cooking over medium heat, stirring occasionally to prevent candy from sticking, until mixture reaches the soft ball stage (236°).

Remove from heat. Add butter without stirring; cool to lukewarm (110°).

Add vanilla; beat until candy loses its gloss and starts to thicken. Pour into lightly buttered 8½ × 4½ × 2½″ loaf pan. Sprinkle top with nuts and gently press them into candy with spoon.

When cool and firm, cut in 32 pieces. Makes about 1¼ pounds.

## FROSTED COFFEE FUDGE

*Unusual mocha-flavored sweetness—pretty to look at, good to eat*

3 c. sugar
2 tblsp. instant coffee powder
⅛ tsp. salt
¾ c. milk
½ c. light cream
1 tblsp. light corn syrup
2 tblsp. butter or margarine
1 tsp. vanilla
1 (6 oz.) pkg. chocolate chips
¼ c. chopped walnuts

Combine sugar, coffee powder, salt, milk, cream and corn syrup in 3-qt. heavy saucepan (buttered). Bring mixture to boil over low heat, stirring constantly. If sugar crystals form on sides of pan, wipe them off. Cook, without stirring, over low heat to the soft ball stage (236°).

Remove from heat; add butter and vanilla; do not stir. Cool, without stirring, until lukewarm (110°).

Beat until candy begins to thicken; pour into buttered 8" square pan.

Melt chocolate chips in top of double boiler over hot (not boiling) water. Spread evenly over cooled fudge; sprinkle with nuts; cut in 36 pieces.

NOTE: This fudge is not recommended for packing and shipping.

## BLOND FUDGE SUPREME

*Serve this blond candy with dark chocolate fudge for color contrast*

| | |
|---|---|
| 3 c. sugar | 3 tblsp. butter or margarine |
| ¾ c. milk | 2 tsp. vanilla |
| 3 tblsp. light corn syrup | 1 c. coarsely chopped nuts |
| ⅛ tsp. salt | |

Combine sugar, milk, corn syrup and salt in 3-qt. heavy saucepan. Cook over medium heat, stirring until sugar dissolves. If sugar crystals form on sides of pan, wipe them off. Cook at a fairly low boil to the soft ball stage (236°). Add butter without stirring; cool to lukewarm (110°).

Add vanilla and beat until candy loses its gloss and starts to thicken. Stir in nuts. Pour at once into a lightly buttered 8" square pan. While warm, mark in 36 pieces. Cool until firm, then cut. Makes 2 pounds.

## Variations

**Coconut Blond Fudge**  Substitute ¾ to 1 c. flaked coconut for the nuts.

**Chocolate Fudge Supreme**  Follow recipe for Blond Fudge Supreme, decreasing corn syrup to 2 tblsp. and vanilla to 1 tsp. Add 2 squares unsweetened chocolate, broken in pieces, to the sugar, milk, corn syrup and salt and cook, stirring constantly, until sugar dissolves. Then follow directions for Blond Fudge Supreme.

**CHRISTMAS FUDGE**

*Delicious light brown candy dotted with red cherries and lots of nuts, including shaved Brazils—a big recipe for a Christmas special*

3 c. sugar  
1½ c. light cream  
1 c. light corn syrup  
1 tsp. salt  
2 tsp. vanilla

1 c. diced candied pineapple  
1 c. halved candied cherries  
1½ c. shaved Brazil nuts  
1½ c. broken walnuts  
2 c. pecan halves

Combine sugar, cream, corn syrup and salt in 3-qt. heavy saucepan. Cook and stir over medium heat until sugar is dissolved. Cover saucepan and boil 1 minute (this helps prevent sugar crystals from forming). Uncover and cook at steady, medium boil to the soft ball stage (236°).

Remove from heat. Add vanilla and immediately beat with electric mixer at medium speed. Beat until mixture is creamy and begins to hold its shape, about 10 minutes.

Thoroughly mix in pineapple, cherries, Brazil nuts, walnuts and pecans.

Press into 2 buttered 9″ square pans. Chill until firm enough to cut. Let stand in refrigerator 24 hours before serving. Makes about 128 pieces, or 4 pounds.

## Remarkable Buttermilk Candy

Recipes for buttermilk candy are going the rounds in country neighborhoods. When a Missouri farmer's wife introduced it to guests at a club meeting, she said: "There's an unusual ingredient in my candy. See if you can guess what it is."

Everyone was curious, but the hostess had to tell about the buttermilk. "You know what happened then," one of the guests reported. "We started looking for paper and pens. Our hostess read the recipe and we all returned home in a candy-making mood. I've been making Buttermilk Candy ever since. You will, too, once you try it."

## BUTTERMILK CANDY

*Try this country relative of fudge and see why it's so popular*

| | |
|---|---|
| 1 c. buttermilk | ¼ c. butter or margarine |
| 1 tsp. baking soda | (½ stick) |
| 2 c. sugar | 1 c. chopped pecans |
| 2 tblsp. light corn syrup | |

Combine buttermilk and baking soda in 3-qt. heavy saucepan. Let stand 20 minutes.

Add sugar and corn syrup to buttermilk. Bring to a boil, stirring until sugar is dissolved. When mixture boils, add butter and cook, stirring occasionally if necessary, to the soft ball stage (236 to 238°) —it will turn a medium brown color.

Remove from heat and cool to lukewarm (110°).

Beat until mixture loses its gloss and starts to thicken. Stir in pecans. Turn into buttered 8″ square pan. Cool until firm; then cut in 36 pieces. Makes about 1½ pounds.

# Yankee-Style Maple Syrup Fudge

If you've ever stood near a Vermont sugar house in late winter or early spring and poured hot maple syrup over fresh-fallen snow packed firmly in a soup plate, you know the delight of eating sugar snow. But even if you live far from New England, you can experience a maple taste treat. Just make a pan of Maple Syrup Fudge. You can follow a recipe that won a prize in the Vermont Farm Bureau's maple syrup recipe contest. That's what our recipe testers did. And they were enthusiastic about the results.

The Vermont farmer's wife who mailed the recipe to us wrote: "After enjoying this fudge myself, and noticing how quickly it became my family's favorite homemade candy, I know other people will love to make and eat it. I'm glad to pass the recipe along." With pride in another native food, she added: "Vermonters prefer butternuts in their Maple Syrup Fudge, but you can use walnuts."

## MAPLE SYRUP FUDGE

*This comes from Vermont sugar bush country direct to your kitchen*

| | |
|---|---|
| 2 c. maple syrup | 1 tsp. vanilla |
| 1 tblsp. light corn syrup | ½ c. chopped walnuts |
| ¾ c. light cream or dairy half-and-half | |

Combine maple syrup, corn syrup and cream in 2-qt. heavy saucepan and place over low heat. Stir constantly until mixture begins to boil; continue cooking without stirring to the soft ball stage (236°).

Remove from heat; cool to lukewarm (110°) without stirring or beating.

Beat with electric mixer on low speed until candy loses its gloss and thickens. (This takes quite a while.)

Stir in vanilla and nuts; pour into lightly buttered 8½ × 4½ × 2½" loaf pan. When cool, cut in 21 pieces. Makes about 1 pound

# Marvelous Burnt Sugar Fudge

Caramelized sugar is legendary in country kitchens, in frosting and fabulous burnt sugar cakes. We give you recipes for candies to which it adds fascinating flavor—Burnt Sugar Fudge, Mexican Orange Candy (recipes follow) and Oklahoma Brown Candy (see Index).

The trick in caramelizing sugar is to melt it, but not to let it scorch. It's really not burnt sugar, but melted or liquefied sugar. Stir sugar constantly while it melts, then take it from the heat, continuing to stir until the lumps, if any, dissolve. It will turn a pale to medium golden brown.

The Kansas farm woman who sent us the following recipe writes: "At evening gatherings, our groups especially enjoy Burnt Sugar Fudge. It appeals to teens who have to be careful about eating chocolate.

"This is a large recipe, resulting in enough leftover candy to take to the teacher next morning. We enjoy using and eating different nuts in the fudge. Sometimes I add almonds, other times cashews. We also like to substitute toasted sunflower seeds for the nuts."

## BURNT SUGAR FUDGE

*No one ever invented caramel flavor to equal that of melted sugar*

6 c. sugar
2 c. dairy half-and-half or
   light cream
¼ tsp. baking soda

½ c. butter (1 stick)
1 tsp. vanilla
2 c. chopped pecans

Put 2 c. sugar in heavy skillet; melt over low heat until sugar liquefies and turns a light golden brown. (Use care not to scorch.)

Combine remaining 4 c. sugar and half-and-half in 3-qt. heavy saucepan. Bring to a boil, stirring constantly. Then slowly pour the melted sugar from skillet into mixture in saucepan. Cook, stirring constantly, to the soft ball stage (238°).

Remove from heat and vigorously stir in baking soda. Mixture will foam. Add butter without stirring. Let stand until lukewarm (110°). Add vanilla and beat until mixture loses its gloss. Stir in nuts. Beat until mixture thickens. Pour into buttered 13×9×2″ pan. When firm, cut in 96 pieces. Makes about 3½ pounds.

## MEXICAN ORANGE CANDY

*Orange and caramel flavors blended . . . no wonder it's so good*

3 c. sugar
1½ c. milk
Grated peel of 1 orange

⅛ tsp. salt
½ c. butter (1 stick)
1 c. chopped nuts

Melt 1 c. sugar over medium heat in 4-qt. heavy saucepan, stirring constantly.

Meanwhile, scald milk in top of double boiler.

When sugar is melted to a light golden brown, take pan off heat and pour the milk into it all at one time. Stir mixture quickly; it foams up (a deep kettle is desirable).

Return pan to heat, add remaining 2 c. sugar and cook, stirring constantly, until sugar dissolves. Continue cooking to the soft ball stage (238°). Remove from heat; add orange peel, salt and butter, but do not stir. Let stand until lukewarm (110°).

Beat until mixture loses its gloss and starts to thicken. Add nuts; stir to mix, then pour into a lightly buttered 9″ square pan. Mark in 49 pieces while warm; when cool and firm, cut. Makes 2 pounds.

N O T E : For a more pronounced orange flavor, popular with our neighbors to the south, use grated peel of 2 oranges.

# Newer Fudge Varieties

Traditional fudge tastes so good that it has inspired the search for easier ways to make equally good candies. New methods and ingredients have led to the discovery of many excellent recipes that have just about eliminated the three once-upon-a-time fudge-making bugaboos: too soft to eat, too hard to handle and—worst of all—"sugary."

Notice the ingredients in the recipes that follow—you'll see evaporated milk in many of them. It is a key to smooth fudge. The availability of semisweet and sweet chocolate, once used only by professionals, is another. And marshmallow creme makes an almost foolproof base. Cream cheese appears as the star ingredient in uncooked fudge, as does sweetened condensed milk.

Today's appliances also influence the recipes. Electric Skillet Peanut Fudge and Double Boiler Fudge are two good examples. And the electric mixer takes over the work in Mother-Son Chocolate Fudge.

You'll find that quite a few recipes make big batches of candy. Those for Superior, Best-Ever, Prize-Winning and Mother-Son Chocolate Fudges yield from 4 to 5½ pounds of candy, for instance. These and other creamy fudges are experienced world-wide travelers, for, like a mother's love, they journey from home kitchens to young men in military service around the globe and to students away at college.

Several recipes less critical than the traditional fudges specify the number of minutes to boil the cooking candy rather than designating the degrees on a thermometer. Watch the clock—it's only a matter of 5 to 7 minutes. Stir the mixture as it cooks, when necessary, to prevent scorching. And do beat the candy long enough. True, the newer fudges are easier to make, but these few rules are the successful route to rich creamy fudge that melts deliciously in the mouth.

## BEST-EVER CHOCOLATE FUDGE

*Milk chocolate gives this big batch of moist fudge its special taste*

1 c. butter or margarine
(2 sticks)
4½ c. sugar
1 (7 oz.) jar marshmallow
creme (about 2 c.)
1 (14½ oz.) can evaporated
milk (1⅔ c.)

8 (1½ oz.) milk chocolate bars,
broken in pieces
1 (12 oz.) pkg. chocolate chips
2 c. chopped walnuts

Combine butter, sugar, marshmallow creme and evaporated milk in 3-qt. heavy saucepan. Bring to a boil over medium to low heat, stirring constantly until sugar dissolves. Boil steadily over low heat 7 minutes, stirring occasionally. Keep mixture at a fairly low boil all the time. The saucepan will be almost full of the cooking mixture.

Remove from heat. Add milk chocolate bars, chocolate chips and nuts; stir until chocolate is melted and blended into mixture.

Pour at once into 2 lightly buttered 9″ square pans. While warm, mark candy in each pan in 64 pieces, or pieces the size you like; when cool and firm, cut. Makes about 5½ pounds.

## SUPERIOR CHOCOLATE FUDGE

*This keeps well if you give it a chance—hide it in a cool place*

4 c. sugar
1 (14½ oz.) can evaporated
milk (1⅔ c.)
1 c. butter or margarine
(2 sticks)

1 (12 oz.) pkg. chocolate chips
1 (7 oz.) jar marshmallow
creme (about 2 c.)
1 tsp. vanilla
1 c. broken walnuts or pecans

Combine sugar, evaporated milk and butter in 3-qt. heavy saucepan. Cook over low heat, stirring frequently, to the soft ball stage (236°). It is important to stir frequently while cooking because mixture scorches easily.

Remove from heat; add chocolate chips, marshmallow creme, vanilla and nuts. Beat until chocolate melts and blends into mixture.

Pour into lightly buttered 9″ square pan. While warm, mark in 36 or 49 pieces with knife; when cool and firm, cut. Makes about 4 pounds.

# Satiny-Smooth Chocolate Fudge

We named this candy for an Illinois farmer's wife and her son. When she sent the recipe, which she originally obtained from her Home Economics Extension Adviser, she said her son often successfully makes the fudge.

Follow the recipe for Mother-Son Chocolate Fudge—especially keep the syrup boiling steadily the full 6 minutes. Cook it a few seconds longer on extremely humid days. This fudge is soft within and firm on the outside after you let it stand in a cold place several hours or overnight. The Illinois contributor of the recipe says she has sent the fudge to Germany and that at the end of the journey, it was soft and creamy. And yes, 3 *tablespoons* of vanilla is the correct amount.

## MOTHER-SON CHOCOLATE FUDGE

*The electric mixer does the beating for this big batch of candy*

| | |
|---|---|
| 4½ c. sugar | 3 (6 oz.) pkgs. chocolate chips |
| 1 (14½ oz.) can evaporated | 1 c. butter (2 sticks) |
| milk (1⅔ c.) | 3 tblsp. vanilla |

Combine sugar and evaporated milk in 3-qt. heavy saucepan. Stir and cook over medium heat until mixture reaches a full rolling boil. Reduce heat if necessary, but keep mixture boiling steadily for 6 minutes. Stir as needed to prevent scorching.

Meanwhile put chocolate chips, butter and vanilla in large bowl of electric mixer.

Pour the hot mixture into electric mixer bowl and beat at high speed until there is no butter on top. To tell when candy is ready to pour, lift beaters and let a little candy drop off them. If the drops do not sink into the candy, it is ready to pour.

Pour into a lightly buttered 9" square pan. Mark in 64 pieces while still warm; let cool several hours or overnight, or until firm, before cutting. (The candy is about 1¼" thick. If you like thinner pieces, use a 13×9×2" buttered pan instead of the 9" square one.) Makes about 4 pounds.

NOTE: If pools of butter form on top as the candy cools, beat it more.

**PRIZE-WINNING FUDGE**

*Rich chocolate flavor is one reason this candy wins blue ribbons*

1 (12 oz.) pkg. chocolate chips
3 (4 oz.) bars sweet cooking
   chocolate
1 (7 oz.) jar marshmallow
   creme (about 2 c.)
4½ c. sugar

⅛ tsp. salt
2 tblsp. butter or margarine
1 (14½ oz.) can evaporated
   milk (1⅔ c.)
2 c. chopped walnuts

Put chocolate chips, cooking chocolate and marshmallow creme in bowl.

Combine sugar, salt, butter and evaporated milk in 3-qt. heavy saucepan. Bring to a boil, stirring until sugar dissolves. Boil steadily over medium heat 6 minutes (keep boiling all the time). Stir constantly to prevent scorching.

Pour boiling syrup over chocolate and marshmallow creme in bowl; beat until chocolate is melted. Stir in walnuts.

Pour into a lightly buttered 13×9×2″ pan. Let cool until firm. Cut in 77 or the desired number of pieces. When cold, pack in airtight containers and store in a cold place. Makes about 5 pounds.

## Fudge That Travels

Delicious and easy to make—that's the recommendation an Iowa farmer's wife sent with her recipe for Serviceman's Special Fudge. She was mailing it frequently to a son in military service in the Orient. The candy is a marshmallow-nut-chocolate fudge that also contains graham cracker crumbs.

When this mother makes the candy for mailing, she pours it into disposable foil pans and does not cut it in pieces. She mails the candy in the pans, which she wraps tightly in foil and then puts in a sturdy box. It arrives thousands of miles from her kitchen in good condition, she knows. Her son always writes a thank-you letter with such comments as: "Mom, that candy you sent was great. It tasted like home and that means good."

## SERVICEMAN'S SPECIAL FUDGE

*It travels to faraway places with cheerful greetings from home*

2 c. sugar
1 c. dairy half-and-half or
  light cream
1 tblsp. butter or margarine
1½ squares unsweetened
  chocolate, cut in pieces

2 tsp. vanilla
1 (1 lb.) pkg. marshmallows,
  cut up (about 8 c.)
1 c. chopped walnuts
3 c. graham cracker crumbs

Combine sugar, half-and-half, butter and chocolate in 3-qt. heavy saucepan. Bring to a boil over medium heat, stirring constantly until sugar dissolves. Continue cooking over low heat to the soft ball stage (236°).

Immediately stir in vanilla, marshmallows, nuts and graham cracker crumbs. Pour into a buttered 13×9×2" pan. (The candy will appear somewhat sticky when you put it in the pan.) Let set until firm. Cut in 77 pieces, or if mailing, do not cut. Makes about 3½ pounds.

## NO-FAIL FUDGE

*Tastes great and it's easy to make*

1 (6 oz.) can evaporated milk
  (⅔ c.)
1⅔ c. sugar
½ tsp. salt

1½ c. cut-up marshmallows
1 (6 oz.) pkg. chocolate chips
1 tsp. vanilla

Combine milk, sugar and salt in 2-qt. heavy saucepan. Cook over medium heat, stirring until sugar dissolves. Bring to a boil and boil steadily 5 minutes, stirring constantly. Remove from heat.

Add marshmallows, chocolate chips and vanilla at once. Stir vigorously for 1 minute, or until marshmallows melt.

Pour into lightly buttered 8" square pan; cool slightly and cut in 36 pieces. Makes 1¾ pounds.

N O T E : To dress up candy for bazaar sales, sprinkle crushed red and white peppermint candy over the top when you pour it into pan.

## MARSHMALLOW FUDGE

*Very easy to make and good to eat—electric mixer does the work*

½ c. butter or margarine
  (1 stick)
⅛ tsp. salt
1 (6 oz.) can evaporated milk
  (⅔ c.)
2¼ c. sugar

1 (8 oz.) pkg. marshmallows
1 (6 oz.) pkg. chocolate chips
1 square semisweet chocolate,
  cut in pieces
1 tsp. vanilla
½ c. chopped nuts

Combine butter, salt, evaporated milk and sugar in 2-qt. heavy saucepan. Stir and bring to a boil; then continue cooking at a steady low boil 8½ minutes, stirring constantly.

Meanwhile, combine marshmallows, chocolate chips, chocolate and vanilla. Pour hot candy over mixture and blend with electric mixer. Add nuts.

Pour into buttered 9" square pan; cool. Cut in 1" squares. Makes 81 pieces, or about 2½ pounds.

## CONFECTIONERS SUGAR FUDGE

*So tempting few people can resist it*

2 (1 lb.) pkgs. confectioners
  sugar
2 (6 oz.) cans evaporated milk
  (1⅓ c.)

2 tblsp. butter
2 (6 oz.) pkgs. chocolate chips
6 tblsp. marshmallow creme
1 c. chopped nuts

Combine sugar, milk and butter in 3-qt. heavy saucepan. Bring to a boil, stirring constantly. Boil 4 minutes.

Add chocolate chips and marshmallow creme. Beat until chocolate melts and fudge thickens. Add nuts.

Turn into buttered 8" square pan. When cool and firm, cut in 36 or 49 pieces. Makes about 3 pounds.

## QUICK CHOCOLATE FUDGE

*It tastes like candy the experts make, and it's failure-proof*

3 tblsp. butter or margarine
3 tblsp. water
1 (14 oz.) pkg. chocolate fudge
  frosting mix

½ c. chopped or broken walnuts
  or pecans

Put butter and water in top of double boiler. Heat until butter melts. Blend in frosting mix until mixture is smooth.

Cook over rapidly boiling water 5 minutes, stirring occasionally. Stir in nuts. Pour into buttered 9×5×3″ loaf pan. Let cool until firm. Cut in 32 pieces. Makes about 1 pound.

## Variations

**Quick Nut Clusters** Omit chopped nuts from Quick Chocolate Fudge. Stir in 2 c. pecan or walnut halves or whole almonds. Instead of pouring into pan, drop from teaspoon onto waxed paper. Cool until firm. Makes about 40 clusters, or 1½ pounds.

**Quick Marshmallow Fudge** Follow recipe for Quick Chocolate Fudge, but add 1 c. miniature marshmallows with the chopped nuts. Pour into loaf pan to cool, then cut in 32 pieces.

## DOUBLE BOILER CHOCOLATE FUDGE

*Candy with a different texture; a splendid stuffing for pitted dates*

| | |
|---|---|
| ¼ c. butter or margarine (½ stick) | ⅓ c. nonfat dry milk powder |
| | ½ c. light corn syrup |
| 3 squares unsweetened chocolate, cut in pieces | 1 tblsp. water |
| | 1 tsp. vanilla |
| 1 lb. confectioners sugar | ½ c. chopped nuts |

Melt butter and chocolate in top of 2-qt. double boiler, or in saucepan over hot water.

Meanwhile, sift together confectioners sugar and dry milk powder; set aside.

Stir corn syrup, water and vanilla into chocolate mixture over hot water. Blend in sugar-dry milk mixture, half at a time, stirring until well blended and smooth.

Remove from boiling water. Stir in nuts. Turn into lightly buttered 8″ square pan. Cool, then cut in 36 pieces. Makes about 2 pounds.

## Variations

**Double Boiler Blond Fudge** Omit chocolate and water from Double Boiler Chocolate Fudge. Increase vanilla from 1 tsp. to 2 tsp.

**Double Boiler Brown Sugar Fudge** Omit chocolate and water from Double Boiler Chocolate Fudge. Melt ½ c. brown sugar with butter and use dark rather than light corn syrup.

**Double Boiler Peanut Fudge**  Omit chocolate and water from Double Boiler Chocolate Fudge. Melt ⅓ c. smooth or crunchy peanut butter with the butter.

**Double Boiler Marshmallow Fudge**  Substitute 1 c. miniature or cut-up marshmallows for chopped nuts in Double Boiler Chocolate Fudge.

## DATE/NUT FUDGE

*For a change, shape candy in balls and roll in finely chopped nuts*

| | |
|---|---|
| 4 c. sugar | 2 tblsp. butter or margarine |
| 1 (14½ oz.) can evaporated milk (1⅔ c.) | 2 tsp. vanilla |
| 2 tblsp. light corn syrup | ½ c. chopped walnuts |
| 1 (8 oz.) pkg. pitted dates, cut up (1 c.) | |

Combine sugar, evaporated milk and corn syrup in 3-qt. heavy saucepan. Cook over medium heat, stirring to dissolve sugar, until mixture reaches boiling point. Add dates and cook over low heat, stirring to prevent scorching, until mixture reaches the soft ball stage (236°). Remove from heat.

Add butter without stirring; cool to lukewarm (110°). Add vanilla and beat until mixture becomes creamy and thickens.

Pour at once into a lightly buttered 9″ square pan. Sprinkle with nuts, gently pressing them into candy. Mark in 49 pieces; when cool and firm, cut. Makes 2½ pounds.

# Four Fudges from One Recipe

You can increase the appeal of any gift box or plate of homemade candy by including a few variations in the shape and/or color of the pieces. For white notes, White Almond and Coconut White Fudges fill the bill splendidly. And Cherry/Date White Fudge charms everyone who sees and tastes. Chocolate/Walnut Fudge, tempting balls rolled in chocolate shot, is irresistible. Fortunately, the electric mixer does the work in making these uncooked candies. The creamy richness comes from cream cheese. Even though the sweets are easy to make, the woman who fixes them gets generous bouquets from everyone who samples. The candies *taste that good!*

## WHITE ALMOND FUDGE

*Easy to make—no cooking, testing for doneness or beating by hand*

| | |
|---|---|
| 1 (3 oz.) pkg. cream cheese | ½ c. chopped almonds |
| 2½ c. sifted confectioners sugar | ⅛ tsp. salt |
| ¼ to ½ tsp. almond extract | |

Beat cream cheese until smooth and soft with electric mixer set at cream (or beat with a spoon). Then slowly blend in remaining ingredients.

Press into a buttered 9×5×3″ loaf pan. Chill until firm, then cut in 21 pieces. Makes about 1 pound.

## *Variations*

**Chocolate/Walnut Fudge** Add 2 squares semisweet chocolate, melted, to cream cheese in White Almond Fudge. When creamed, slowly blend in 2 c. sifted confectioners sugar, ½ tsp. vanilla, ½ c. chopped walnuts and ⅛ tsp. salt. Shape 1 tsp. candy into ball and drop into small bowl containing ⅓ c. (2 oz.) chocolate shot (jimmies). Roll ball in chocolate shot and place on waxed paper or buttered foil. Repeat until all candy is shaped in balls. Makes 30 balls.

**Cherry/Date White Fudge** Substitute ¼ c. cut-up dates (snip fine with scissors) and ¼ c. cut-up candied cherries for almonds in White Almond Fudge. Use ¼ tsp. almond extract or ½ tsp. vanilla. Makes 21 pieces.

**Coconut White Fudge** Substitute ½ c. flaked or cookie coconut for almonds in White Almond Fudge. Makes 21 pieces.

## CREAM CHEESE FUDGE

*Excellent fudge without cooking—it's rich, luscious and creamy*

| | |
|---|---|
| 1 (3 oz.) pkg. cream cheese, softened | ½ tsp. vanilla |
| 1 tblsp. milk | ⅛ tsp. salt |
| 2 c. unsifted confectioners sugar | 1 c. chopped nuts |
| 2 squares unsweetened chocolate, melted | |

Combine cheese and milk; beat until smooth. Gradually beat in sugar; then blend in melted chocolate. Stir in vanilla, salt and nuts.

Press into a lightly buttered 8" square pan. Mark in 24 pieces. Chill until firm, then cut. Makes 1 pound.

# Popular Cheddar Cheese Fudge

Cheese fudge proves the inaccuracy of the old saying that there is nothing new under the sun. When a state supervisor of the school lunch program made some of this candy for one of our food editors, she removed any question there might have been about why the sweet was so popular with youngsters.

One of the splendid features of the candy, loaded with Cheddar cheese and dry milk powder, flavored with butter, vanilla and cocoa, is that the electric mixer does almost all the work. You do not even cook the fudge. It's ideal for serving to a crowd of youngsters. But pass it to grownups, too, for they'll like its creaminess, sweet chocolate flavor and the way it serves as a snack to satisfy appetites.

## CHEDDAR CHEESE FUDGE

*Cheese flavor is subtle in this creamy, no-cook, protein-rich candy*

2 c. shredded Cheddar cheese (½ lb.)
1 c. butter (2 sticks)
½ c. cocoa

1½ lbs. confectioners sugar
1½ c. nonfat dry milk powder (½ lb.)
½ tblsp. vanilla

Have all ingredients at room temperature; combine in large mixer bowl. Beat until creamy (it may be necessary to moisten mixture with ¼ c. whole milk).

Put in buttered 9" square pan; chill. When firm, cut candy in 64 squares. Makes about 3½ pounds.

N O T E : Drained maraschino cherries, flaked coconut, miniature marshmallows or chopped nuts may be added.

## MARSHMALLOW/BUTTERSCOTCH FUDGE

*Takes little time to make this candy*

1 (6 oz.) pkg. chocolate chips
1 (6 oz.) pkg. butterscotch-
  flavored morsels
1 c. chopped nuts
12 large marshallows, cut up
  (with scissors)

2 c. sugar
¾ c. evaporated milk
1 tblsp. butter

Combine chocolate and butterscotch pieces and nuts in bowl.
Set aside.

Combine marshmallows, sugar, evaporated milk (store leftover
evaporated milk in refrigerator) and butter in 2-qt. heavy saucepan. Bring to a boil over medium heat, stirring constantly. Continue
to boil 6 minutes, stirring to prevent scorching. Remove from heat.

Add first mixture and beat until candy thickens and is creamy.
Turn at once into lightly buttered 8″ square pan. When firm, cut
in 36 pieces. Makes about 2¼ pounds.

## Compromise Peanut/Chocolate Fudge

Some exciting things come out of friendly family arguments. Peanut/
Chocolate Sandwiches, for instance! A California rancher's wife
says every time she used to get ready to make fudge the family
was divided on the kind they wanted—chocolate or peanut butter.
Being the diplomat that most mothers are, she worked out a com-
promise that pleases everyone—Peanut/Chocolate Sandwiches.

She says that often instead of dropping the candy and peanut
butter from a spoon, she pours half the fudge mixture into a foil-
lined 8″ square pan, dots the top with peanut butter, swirls it
around and then spreads on the remaining half of the chocolate
fudge. While still warm, she marks the pieces and cuts them when
the candy is cold and firm.

She lines the pan with foil, not to save on dishwashing, but to
free it for more candy. Her family and friends like the fudge so
much that, by the time the first batch is cool, she frequently
has a second panful ready to pour.

## PEANUT/CHOCOLATE SANDWICHES

*Work fast when you drop the candy; better still, let someone help*

1 (6 oz.) can evaporated milk
(⅔ c.)
1½ c. sugar
1 (6 oz.) pkg. chocolate chips
⅓ c. butter or margarine

1 tsp. vanilla
⅓ c. finely chopped salted
peanuts
½ c. peanut butter (about)

Combine evaporated milk and sugar in 3-qt. heavy saucepan. Cook over medium heat, stirring constantly, until sugar dissolves. Bring to a boil and boil 7 minutes. (Keep mixture at a steady, fairly low boil. Stir only to prevent candy from sticking to pan.)

Remove from heat and add chocolate chips and butter. Beat until smooth. Stir in vanilla and peanuts.

Drop from tablespoon onto foil-lined baking sheet to make 24 candies; save about ½ c. mixture to top candy drops. Put about 1 tsp. peanut butter on top each chocolate drop, then drop remaining chocolate mixture on top of peanut butter. Work fast. Makes 24 pieces, about 1¾ pounds.

## ELECTRIC SKILLET PEANUT FUDGE

*Treat peanut butter fans with this candy—it's a fast-fix, tasty sweet*

2 c. sugar
3 tblsp. butter or margarine
1 c. evaporated milk
1 c. miniature marshmallows

1 (12 oz.) jar crunchy peanut
butter
1 tsp. vanilla

Set electric skillet at 340°. Add sugar, butter and evaporated milk (store leftover evaporated milk in refrigerator). Stir until mixture comes to a boil. Start counting time; boil mixture 5 minutes, stirring constantly. Turn off skillet heat.

Add marshmallows, peanut butter and vanilla. Stir until marshmallows and peanut butter melt and blend into candy. Pour into lightly buttered 8" square pan. Cool, then cut in 36 pieces. Makes 2 pounds.

## DANISH FUDGE

*Teen-age candy makers like this fudge that you beat without cooling*

¾ c. butter (1½ sticks)
1 lb. brown sugar
1 (6 oz.) can evaporated milk
(⅔ c.)
1 lb. less ¼ c. confectioners
sugar

1 tsp. vanilla
1 c. broken pecans, walnuts or
peanuts

Melt butter in 3-qt. heavy saucepan. Add brown sugar and evaporated milk; stir to blend. Bring to a boil and boil exactly 3 minutes. Remove from heat and let cool 2 minutes. If sugar crystals form on sides of pan, wipe them off.

Meanwhile, sift confectioners sugar; beat it into mixture until candy is well blended. Add vanilla and nuts; mix to distribute.

Pour into buttered 9″ square pan. Mark in squares. Chill; cut in pieces, place in airtight container and refrigerate. Candy will keep for several weeks. Makes about 81 squares, or 2¾ pounds.

## GOLDEN CARAMEL FUDGE

*Velvety smooth and rich in flavor; it's a breeze to make*

2 tblsp. butter or margarine
2 tblsp. plus 1 tsp. water
1 (13 oz.) pkg. caramel
frosting mix

½ c. chopped pecans

Put butter and water in top of double boiler. Heat until butter melts. Add frosting mix; stir until mixture is smooth.

Cook over boiling water 5 minutes, stirring occasionally. Stir in pecans. Pour into buttered 9×5×3″ loaf pan. Let cool until firm, then cut in 32 pieces. Makes about 1 pound.

## Variation

**Quick Pralines** Omit chopped nuts from Golden Caramel Fudge. Stir in 1 c. pecan halves. Drop from teaspoon onto waxed paper. Makes about 36 pralines.

## QUICK 'N EASY FUDGE

*Let the children make this fudge—it's cream-colored and velvety*

3 tblsp. butter or margarine          32 pecan halves
3 tblsp. milk
1 (14 oz.) pkg. white frosting
    mix

Put butter and milk in top of double boiler. Heat over hot water until butter melts. Add the frosting mix and stir until mixture is smooth and blended. Then heat over rapidly boiling water 5 minutes, stirring occasionally.

Pour into buttered 9×5×3" loaf pan and at once press pecan halves into top of candy. (Do this while candy is warm or nuts will not stay in place when candy is cut.)

Cool until candy is firm. Cut in 32 pieces so there is a pecan half on top of each. Makes about 1 pound.

## *Variations*

**Peppermint Patties**  Follow recipe for Quick 'n Easy Fudge, but omit nuts. Add ½ tsp. peppermint extract and 3 to 4 drops red or green food color to the hot candy. Keep candy over hot water and drop from teaspoon onto waxed paper, making rounded, but flat patties. While still warm, press tines of table fork across tops of patties to make a "ribbed" design. Makes about 48 patties.

**Lemon Patties**  Follow recipe for Quick 'n Easy Fudge, substituting 1 (13 oz.) pkg. lemon creamy-type frosting mix for the white frosting mix. Make like Peppermint Patties, adding ½ tsp. lemon extract instead of the peppermint, and yellow food color instead of red or green. Makes 48 patties.

**Quick Lemon Fudge**  Follow recipe for Quick 'n Easy Fudge, but substitute 1 (13 oz.) pkg. lemon creamy-type frosting mix for the white frosting mix.

# Elegant Italian Cream Fudge

This creamy candy containing crisp nuts is a second generation recipe. The Indiana homemaker who passes it on to you inherited it, and the memory of the marvelous candy, from her mother. Now she makes it in her own kitchen at Christmas time or whenever she wants a big batch of candy.

Be prepared to stand over it while cooking. The mixture is thick and it sticks to the pan unless your spoon keeps it moving. And when you beat the lukewarm candy, let your electric mixer do the work. "My mother always made sure there were at least two of us on hand to help with the beating," the Indiana homemaker remembers.

If you fear you cannot slice the candy neatly, dismiss your concern. A sharp knife cuts evenly through the whole Brazil nuts, and you have crisp, white nuts in rich brown candy. You can substitute other nuts for those from South America, but the Brazil nuts make the fudge special.

## ITALIAN CREAM FUDGE

*There may be more delicious candy but we've never encountered it*

| | |
|---|---|
| 6 c. sugar | ⅛ tsp. salt |
| 1 (14½ oz.) can evaporated milk (1⅔ c.) | 1 c. butter or margarine (2 sticks) |
| 1 (6 oz.) can evaporated milk (⅔ c.) | 1 tblsp. vanilla |
| 2 c. light corn syrup | 3 c. whole Brazil nuts (1 lb.) |

Combine sugar, evaporated milk, corn syrup and salt in 4-qt. heavy saucepan. Cook over medium to low heat, stirring constantly, until mixture reaches the soft ball stage (238°).

Remove from heat and add butter without stirring. Cool to lukewarm (110°).

Add vanilla. Beat with electric mixer at low speed until candy thickens and is very creamy. Stir in nuts quickly. Pour into 2 buttered 8½ × 4½ × 2½″ loaf pans; cool until firm. Remove candy from pans and wrap each loaf in foil or plastic wrap. Store in cold place. When ready to use, cut in thin slices. Makes about 5½ pounds.

## CHRISTMAS CHERRY FUDGE

*Festive bright pink candy—include a few pieces in holiday boxes*

| | |
|---|---|
| 1 (3 oz.) pkg. cherry flavor gelatin | 1½ c. milk |
| | ¼ c. butter (½ stick) |
| 3½ c. sugar | ½ c. chopped candied cherries |
| ¼ tsp. baking soda | ½ c. chopped walnuts |

Combine gelatin, sugar, baking soda and milk in a 3-qt. heavy saucepan. Cook and stir over medium heat until sugar is dissolved. Continue cooking without stirring to the soft ball stage (236°).

Remove from heat; add butter. Pour into a large buttered platter; cool without stirring until mixture is lukewarm. Then beat until mixture loses its gloss.

Quickly stir in cherries and walnuts.

Turn at once into a buttered 8″ square pan. When firm, cut in 2×1″ (about) rectangles. Makes about 28 pieces, or 2¼ pounds.

# Country Kitchen Cream Candies

Among the most velvety, melt-in-the-mouth candies you can cook are the country specials rich and delicious with cream. If you store them in tightly covered containers and place them in a cool place, they'll stay fresh longer than many sweets. The cream prevents them from drying out quickly. It takes little imagination to figure out why they taste extra-good. Few flavors, if any, excel the delicacy of cream in candy.

### LIGHT OPERA CREAMS

*Delicious candy with good keeping qualities—ideal for gift boxes*

| | |
|---|---|
| 2 c. sugar | 1 tblsp. light corn syrup |
| ½ tsp. salt | 1 tsp. vanilla |
| ¾ c. heavy cream | ¾ c. chopped walnuts or pecans |
| ½ c. milk | |

Combine sugar, salt, cream, milk and corn syrup in 2-qt. heavy saucepan. Bring to a boil over low heat, stirring constantly. Continue cooking, stirring often to prevent scorching, until mixture reaches the soft ball stage (238°).

Remove from heat. Wipe pouring edge of pan with damp cloth and pour candy into a clean pan. Cool without stirring to lukewarm (110°).

Add vanilla and beat until candy loses its gloss. Stir in nuts. Pour at once into a lightly buttered 8″ square pan. Mark in 36 pieces while warm; cool until firm, then cut. Makes 1½ pounds.

## Variations

**Grand Operas** When candy (Light Opera Creams) in pan is firm, spread with 4 squares semisweet chocolate, melted. Cool until chocolate topping is firm, then cut in 36 pieces.

**Opera Log** After adding nuts when making Light Opera Creams, beat until you can handle candy. Place on a sheet of foil or waxed paper and shape into a log or roll about 7″ long. Cool. Partially melt 4 squares semisweet chocolate over hot water. Remove from water and stir vigorously until chocolate is melted thoroughly. Then spread some of the chocolate over top and sides of candy log. When firm, turn log and spread bottom with remaining melted chocolate. When firm, slice crosswise in 36 pieces.

## SOUR CREAM CANDY

*Sour cream contributes its flavor to this rich and creamy sweet*

| | |
|---|---|
| 1 c. dairy sour cream | 1 tsp. vanilla |
| 1 c. sugar | ½ c. chopped pecans or black |
| 2 tblsp. butter | walnuts |

Stir sour cream and sugar together in a 2-qt. heavy saucepan. Bring to a boil, stirring constantly, and cook to the soft ball stage (238°). (Stir while cooking to prevent scorching.)

Remove from heat; add butter and cool without stirring or moving until pan feels lukewarm to the hand (110°).

Stir in vanilla and pecans. Beat until candy loses its gloss. Pour and knead into a buttered 8½ × 4½ × 2½″ loaf pan. Chill. Cut in 21 pieces. Makes ¾ pound.

## PEANUT SOUR CREAM CANDY

*You'll hunt a long time before you find a better-tasting sweet*

| | |
|---|---|
| 2 c. sugar | ½ tsp. vanilla |
| ⅛ tsp. salt | 3 drops almond extract |
| 1 c. dairy sour cream | 1 c. peanuts |
| ⅛ tsp. ground cinnamon | |

Mix sugar, salt and cream in 2-qt. heavy saucepan; boil gently, without stirring, to firm ball stage (245°). Cool to lukewarm (110°); add flavorings and beat until creamy.

Fold in peanuts. Pour into buttered 8″ square pan. When cool, cut in squares. Makes 36 squares.

## FAMILY REUNION CREAM CANDY

*End a meal with this caramel-colored candy. Guests will love it*

| | |
|---|---|
| 3 c. sugar | ¼ tsp. salt |
| 1 c. light corn syrup | 1 tsp. vanilla |
| 1½ c. heavy cream | |

Combine sugar, syrup and cream in 3-qt. heavy saucepan. Cook, stirring, until mixture reaches a boil. Add salt and continue cooking to the soft ball stage (238°).

Remove from heat; add vanilla and beat until you can pick up candy in your hands. Knead until smooth and fine in texture.

Store in tightly covered container and place in refrigerator. Candy may be stored several weeks. When ready to serve, shape into rolls or pieces, as directed below. Makes 2¼ pounds.

**Cream Candy Rolls**   Knead ¼ c. finely chopped nuts into half of Family Reunion Cream Candy. Shape into roll 9″ long, 2″ in diameter. Roll in finely chopped nuts. Chill. Slice in 36 pieces at serving time.

**Cream Bonbons**   Shape half of Family Reunion Cream Candy into bonbons, pressing a pecan half on top of each piece. Makes 36 pieces.

## CINNAMON CANDY BALLS

*If you like the cinnamon-sugar taste, here's your candy—it's easy*

| | |
|---|---|
| 2½ c. sugar | 4 drops oil of cinnamon |
| ½ c. light or dark corn syrup | 2 tsp. ground cinnamon |
| 1 c. heavy cream | 2 tsp. sugar (preferably |
| 1 c. dairy half-and-half | superfine) |
| ⅛ tsp. salt | |

Combine 2½ c. sugar, corn syrup, heavy cream, half-and-half and salt in a 3-qt. heavy saucepan. Cook over medium heat to the soft ball stage (238°). Remove from heat and let stand without stirring 15 to 20 minutes.

Add oil of cinnamon; stir well. Continue stirring until mixture thickens.

Meanwhile, combine ground cinnamon and 2 tsp. sugar in a small bowl. With lightly buttered palms pick up a small spoonful of candy and quickly roll into ball between palms. Drop in cinnamon-sugar mixture and roll to coat thoroughly; place on waxed paper. Repeat until all candy is rolled and coated with cinnamon-sugar. Makes 4 to 5 dozen balls, depending on size, or 1½ pounds.

NOTE: If candy begins to harden while rolling into balls, set pan in warm water until candy softens enough to roll.

# Old-Fashioned Penuche

Every woman cherishes a few recipes because they have a special meaning to her. Brown sugar fudge or penuche appears on the list of one of our food editors. She associates it with her mother's kitchen—a saucepan of soft bubbling, low-boiling brown sugar syrup, the mixture beaten to creaminess with plenty of pecans in it, and youngsters gathering round for the first taste.

Sometimes during the cooking, the acid in brown sugar curdles the milk in the candy. If you're a new penuche cook, don't worry: When you beat the cooked and cooled candy before pouring it into a pan, the curdles vanish.

## NUT PENUCHE

*Brown sugar fudge has ardent fans; this is a splendid recipe for it*

1 lb. light brown sugar (2¼ c. firmly packed)
¾ c. milk
⅛ tsp. salt

2½ tblsp. butter or margarine
1 tsp. vanilla
½ c. chopped walnuts or pecans

Combine sugar, milk and salt in 2-qt. heavy saucepan. Place over medium heat, and stir until sugar dissolves. If sugar crystals form on sides of pan, wipe them off. When mixture comes to a boil, cook without stirring until it reaches the soft ball stage (238°). Remove from heat.

Add butter without stirring; cool to lukewarm (110°). Add vanilla; beat until mixture starts to thicken. Add nuts and beat and stir until thick and creamy. Pour at once into greased 9×5×3" loaf pan. (Do not scrape pan.)

Mark in 24 pieces while warm; when cool and firm, cut. Makes about 1¼ pounds.

NOTE: You can substitute 2 c. granulated brown sugar for the 2¼ c. light brown sugar.

## Variation

**Peanut Penuche** Substitute chopped salted peanuts for the walnuts or pecans in Nut Penuche. Omit salt, if using salted peanuts.

## MAPLE PENUCHE

*If they like the maple sugar taste, you'll please them with this*

| | |
|---|---|
| 1½ c. light brown sugar | ¾ c. maple-blended syrup |
| 1 c. white sugar | 2½ tblsp. butter or margarine |
| ¼ tsp. salt | ½ tsp. vanilla |
| ¾ c. milk | |

Combine sugars, salt, milk and maple syrup in 2-qt. heavy saucepan. Place over medium heat, stirring constantly, until sugars dissolve. If sugar crystals form on sides of pan, wipe them off. Continue cooking at fairly slow boil, stirring just enough to prevent scorching, until mixture reaches the soft ball stage (238°). Remove from heat.

Add butter without stirring. Do not move or jar pan. Cool until candy is lukewarm (110°), or until bottom of saucepan feels lukewarm.

Add vanilla and beat until mixture loses its gloss and starts to thicken. When a small amount dropped from the spoon holds its shape, pour at once into a lightly buttered 8" square pan. While still warm, mark in 20 pieces; when cool and firm, cut. Makes 1¼ pounds.

## Variation

**Plantation Penuche** Follow recipe for Maple Penuche but omit maple-blended syrup and use 1½ c. milk instead of ¾ c.

## COFFEE PENUCHE

*Coffee, brown sugar, pecans—no wonder this tastes extra-good*

| | |
|---|---|
| 1 tsp. instant coffee | 3 tblsp. butter |
| ⅔ c. boiling water | 1 tsp. vanilla |
| 2½ c. brown sugar, firmly packed | ½ c. chopped pecans |

Dissolve coffee in boiling water and put with brown sugar in 2-qt. heavy saucepan. Cook over medium heat, stirring constantly, until mixture boils. Continue cooking to the soft ball stage (238°). Remove from heat.

Add butter without stirring and cool to lukewarm (110°).

Add vanilla; beat until mixture loses its gloss and starts to thicken. Quickly stir in nuts. Pour into lightly buttered 8½ ×4½ ×2½″ loaf pan.

Mark in 32 pieces while warm; when cool and firm, cut. Makes about 1½ pounds.

## MEXICAN PENUCHE

*Chocolate does something good to penuche . . . you'll like this*

| | |
|---|---|
| 3 c. dark brown sugar | 1 tblsp. butter |
| 3 tblsp. light corn syrup | 1 tsp. vanilla |
| 1 c. milk | 1½ c. broken nuts |
| ½ square unsweetened chocolate | |

Combine sugar, corn syrup, milk and chocolate in 3-qt. heavy saucepan. Butter sides of pan to help prevent formation of sugar crystals. Bring to a boil and add butter; stir occasionally until candy reaches the soft ball stage (238°).

Remove from heat; let stand 10 minutes. Add vanilla and nuts, mixing in thoroughly. Continue stirring until candy loses its gloss and begins to thicken.

Turn into buttered 9″ square pan; cut in 50 pieces when set. Makes about 1¾ pounds.

# Sauerkraut Candy Comes Back

Most youngsters never heard of Sauerkraut Candy, but oldsters know it well. The "sauerkraut" is shredded coconut and you team it with penuche. Many grocery stores throughout the Midwest sold it from barrels during the Gay Nineties. It held its place in the sun until World War I. Then for some reason it almost disappeared. Make it once and you may stage a revival, for the candy tastes extra-good.

## SAUERKRAUT CANDY

*You can't miss with this combination of lots of coconut in penuche*

2 c. light brown sugar, firmly packed
2 c. white sugar
¼ c. light corn syrup
1⅓ c. dairy half-and-half
¼ c. butter (½ stick)
¼ tsp. salt
1 tsp. vanilla
1½ c. shredded coconut

Combine sugars, corn syrup and half-and-half in 3-qt. heavy saucepan with buttered sides. Cook over medium-high heat, stirring until sugar is dissolved. Continue cooking to the soft ball stage (238 to 240°).

Remove from heat; add butter and salt without stirring. Cool to lukewarm (110°). Add vanilla and beat until creamy; mixture loses gloss and becomes opaque.

Fold in coconut all at once. Pour onto buttered and chilled platter or into an 8″ square pan. Cut in slices if thick or in 49 squares if molded in pan. Makes about 2¼ pounds.

# Divinity and Nougat

Candy clouds of pastel pink and green, maple white or snowy white—that's divinity. No one remembers who first made this candy, but rumors have it that the first bite brought this exclamation: "Why, it's dream-stuff—it's divine!" The beauty and heavenly taste of divinity (which contains no fat) make it a fast seller at food sales and bazaars.

Making divinity is a lot easier than it used to be, for electric mixers now do all or part of the beating. Use the appliance on medium speed, but if the mixture becomes too stiff for the mixer, finish up the beating by hand with a wooden spoon. It is important to beat divinity until it begins to lose its gloss and a small amount, dropped from a spoon, holds a soft peak. Sometimes the beating takes as long as 12 to 15 minutes.

You can drop the beaten candy from a teaspoon onto waxed paper if you work fast. It hardens quickly. If it begins to set before you finish, stir in a few drops of hot water. The candy may look a little rough and irregular—but this is divinity's hallmark. If you have a good helper, you can work together, twice as fast! Some candy makers prefer to pour the beaten divinity into a lightly buttered pan, letting it cool until firm on top (it shouldn't stick to your finger when you press it lightly). Then cut it in pieces. This candy keeps a little better than divinity dropped from a spoon, and the pieces are neat and uniform in size.

Country women often freeze divinity in airtight containers with waxed paper between the layers, although some candy makers first freeze the unwrapped candy and then store it in the freezer in tightly closed plastic bags.

Some women lament that divinity sometimes is temperamental and refuses to harden. If you cook and beat it enough, you should have no difficulty, but if you have trouble, heat it over hot water until a small amount dropped on waxed paper is firm. However, the quality of reheated divinity usually is somewhat below par.

# DIVINITY

*Sells fast at food bazaars*

2¼ c. sugar
⅓ c. white corn syrup
¼ tsp. salt
⅓ c. water

2 egg whites
1 tsp. vanilla
⅔ c. chopped pecans or walnuts

Place sugar, corn syrup, salt and water in a 2-qt. heavy saucepan; cook and stir over high heat until sugar is dissolved. Continue cooking without stirring over medium heat until syrup reaches the hard ball stage (255°). Wipe off any sugar crystals that form on sides of pan.

Meanwhile, beat egg whites until stiff. Pour hot syrup slowly over egg whites and beat on medium speed of mixer until candy fluffs up. Add vanilla and continue beating on medium speed, or by hand, until mixture begins to lose its gloss and a small amount dropped from a spoon holds soft peaks. (If the candy gets too stiff for the mixer, complete the beating with a wooden spoon.) Fold in nuts.

Working quickly, drop candy by teaspoonfuls onto waxed paper or turn into lightly buttered 8″ square pan. If divinity becomes too stiff, stir in a few drops of hot water. Makes about 24 pieces or 1 pound.

## Variations

**Pink Peppermint Drops** Add a few drops red food color and ¼ tsp. peppermint extract with vanilla. Omit nuts and add ¾ c. crushed peppermint stick candy.

**Vanilla/Chocolate Layer** Make Divinity as directed. Pour about half of mixture into a buttered 9×5×3″ loaf pan or baking dish. Fold 1½ squares unsweetened chocolate, melted, into remaining Divinity. Place this mixture on top of vanilla mixture. When set, turn out of pan and cut in 32 pieces.

*Slick Trick:* When you've beaten divinity and it's ready to drop, do it this way. Put divinity into a plastic bag, snip off one corner of the bag and squeeze the candy out onto waxed paper, making attractive pieces with peaks. Not only is this method quicker than dropping candy from a spoon, you will get more uniform-looking pieces.

## RASPBERRY PINK DIVINITY

*Pale pink with faint raspberry flavor—pretty for a bridal shower*

⅔ c. water
¾ c. light corn syrup
2½ c. sugar
⅛ tsp. salt

2 egg whites
2 tblsp. raspberry flavor gelatin
1 c. broken walnuts

Combine water and syrup in 3-qt. heavy saucepan.

Bring to a boil; add sugar and salt and cook, stirring until sugar is dissolved. Continue cooking without stirring to the hard ball stage (256°). If sugar crystals form on sides of pan, wipe them off. Remove from heat.

With electric mixer on medium speed beat egg whites and gelatin in warmed bowl until mixture forms soft peaks.

Pour the hot candy syrup in a fine stream into egg whites, beating constantly. When all the syrup is added, remove beater and beat by hand with wooden spoon until candy starts to lose its gloss and begins to set; it forms soft peaks when dropped from a spoon. Stir in nuts.

Drop from teaspoon onto waxed paper. Work fast for candy hardens quickly. When cool and dry on outside place in airtight container with waxed paper between layers. Store in a cold place, or freeze. Makes about 48 pieces, or 1¾ pounds.

N O T E : You can use lime flavor instead of raspberry flavor gelatin to make a pretty pale green divinity.

## STRAWBERRY DIVINITY

*Bright color and berry flavor make this candy a drawing card*

3 c. sugar
¾ c. light corn syrup
¾ c. water
2 egg whites

1 (3 oz.) pkg. strawberry flavor gelatin
1 c. broken or cut-up nuts

Combine sugar, corn syrup and water in 3-qt. heavy saucepan. Cook over medium heat, stirring constantly until sugar dissolves. If sugar crystals form on sides of pan, wipe them off. Continue cooking to the hard ball stage (252°).

Meanwhile, beat egg whites until stiff, but not dry; blend in gelatin.

When syrup reaches 252°, pour in a thin stream over egg whites, beating constantly with electric mixer on medium speed. Beat as long as possible, using wooden spoon if mixture becomes too stiff for mixer.

Add nuts and pour into lightly buttered 9″ square pan. When cool and firm, cut in 36 pieces. Makes about 2 pounds.

## BROWN SUGAR DIVINITY

*Pecans glorify this creamy candy but walnuts also are good in it*

| | |
|---|---|
| 1 c. light brown sugar, firmly packed | ⅛ tsp. salt |
| | 2 egg whites |
| 1 c. white sugar | 1 tsp. vanilla |
| ⅔ c. water | 1 c. broken pecans |
| ⅓ c. light corn syrup | |

Combine sugars, water, corn syrup and salt in 2-qt. heavy saucepan. Bring to a boil over medium heat, stirring constantly. If sugar crystals form on sides of pan, wipe them off. Boil gently at a fairly low boil without stirring until mixture reaches the hard ball stage (265°).

Just before temperature reaches 265°, beat egg whites with electric mixer until peaks are formed when beater is raised. Beating constantly on medium speed, slowly pour hot syrup in a fine stream into egg whites. Continue beating until mixture starts to lose its gloss. Stir in vanilla and nuts. Spread into a lightly buttered 8″ square pan; when firm, cut in 25 pieces. Makes about 1¼ pounds.

## MAPLE SUGAR DIVINITY

*Off-white in color, superb in taste and luscious with or without nuts*

| | |
|---|---|
| 2⅓ c. sugar | 2 egg whites |
| ½ c. maple syrup | ½ tsp. vanilla |
| ⅔ c. light corn syrup | 1 c. broken pecans or walnuts |
| ¼ c. water | (optional) |
| ¼ tsp. salt | |

Combine sugar, maple syrup, corn syrup, water and salt in 2-qt. heavy saucepan. Cook, stirring until sugar is dissolved. If sugar crystals form on sides of pan, wipe them off. Continue cooking without stirring to the hard ball stage (265°).

Meanwhile, beat egg whites until stiff but not dry. Remove syrup from heat when it reaches 265° and slowly pour over egg whites, beating with electric mixer on medium speed. Continue beating until candy starts to lose its gloss and a little of mixture dropped from a spoon holds its shape.

Add vanilla and nuts and mix in thoroughly. Drop from teaspoon onto waxed paper, or pour into buttered 8″ square pan. When firm, cut in 25 pieces. Makes about 1¼ pounds.

## CHOCOLATE RIPPLE DIVINITY

*Snowy white candy marbled with chocolate—pleases everyone*

| | |
|---|---|
| 2 c. sugar | 2 egg whites |
| ½ c. water | 1 tsp. vanilla |
| ½ c. light corn syrup | 1 (6 oz.) pkg. chocolate chips |
| ⅛ tsp. salt | |

Combine sugar, water, corn syrup and salt in a 2-qt. heavy saucepan. Cook over low heat, stirring constantly until sugar is dissolved. If sugar crystals form on sides of pan, wipe them off. Cook to hard ball stage (252°) without stirring.

Beat egg whites until stiff. Pour hot syrup slowly over egg whites, beating constantly. Add vanilla. Continue beating by hand or with electric mixer on medium speed until mixture begins to lose its gloss and a small amount dropped from a spoon holds soft peaks. (If the candy gets too stiff for the mixer, complete the beating with a wooden spoon.)

Fold in chocolate chips quickly and drop from teaspoon onto buttered waxed paper. Makes 24 pieces, or about 1 pound.

*FOR EVERY OCCASION—See how many candies you can pick out: Chocolate Fudge Velvet, Fruited Sea Foam, Double Divinity, Virginia Peanut Brittle, Christmas Ribbons, American-Style Nougat, Homemade Candy Bars with Caramel Nut filling, Anise Candy, Perfect Butterscotch Patties, Lollypops and Pastel Bonbons. (For recipes, check Index.)*

# Two-Temperature Candy Cooking

Some expert candy makers prefer to divide the cooking of divinity into two parts. First, they cook the syrup to the firm ball stage (248°) and pour about half of it over the egg whites, beating constantly. They cook the remainder of the syrup to the soft crack stage (272°) and slowly pour it into the candy, beating constantly. A candy thermometer and the electric mixer are required for this method.

It's more work to make divinity this way, but some of our taste-testers think the candy is a trifle creamier and softer than divinity cooked to one temperature. You'll want to try our recipes for Double Divinity, either white or chocolate, and colorful Red Hot Divinity to find out which method you think makes the better candy.

## DOUBLE DIVINITY

*A 2-in-1 recipe—will make either chocolate or snowy white candy*

| | |
|---|---|
| 2½ c. sugar | ¼ tsp. salt |
| ½ c. light corn syrup | 2 egg whites |
| ½ c. water | 1 tsp. vanilla |

Combine sugar, corn syrup, water and salt in 2-qt. heavy sauce-pan. Cook over medium heat, stirring constantly until mixture comes to a boil. If sugar crystals form on sides of pan, wipe them off. Reduce heat and cook without stirring until temperature reaches firm ball stage (248°).

Just before candy mixture reaches 248°, beat egg whites until stiff, but not dry. Slowly pour about half of the hot mixture over egg whites, beating constantly with electric mixer at medium speed.

Continue to cook remaining syrup to the soft crack stage (272°). Beating constantly, pour hot mixture, a tablespoonful at a time, over egg white mixture, beating well after each addition. Continue beating until mixture begins to lose its gloss and a small amount dropped from a spoon holds soft peaks. If mixture becomes too stiff for mixer, beat with wooden spoon.

Mix in vanilla. Drop by teaspoonfuls onto waxed paper. Makes 27 drops or 1½ pounds.

NOTE: You can add 1 c. coarsely broken walnuts or pecans to Double Divinity. Mix them in with the vanilla.

## Variation

**Chocolate Divinity** If beating Double Divinity with electric mixer, add 2 squares unsweetened chocolate, melted, immediately after last addition of hot syrup; beat until mixture starts to lose its gloss. If beating by hand, beat 5 minutes after last addition of hot syrup to egg white mixture and then add 2 squares chocolate, melted, and beat until mixture holds its shape when dropped from a spoon.

## RED HOT DIVINITY

*If you enjoy the taste of cinnamon, you'll like this colorful candy*

½ c. small red cinnamon candies  (red hots)
½ c. hot water
½ c. light corn syrup

2 c. sugar
2 egg whites
1 tsp. vanilla

Combine cinnamon candies and water in 2-qt. heavy saucepan; cook until candies dissolve. Add corn syrup and sugar; cook, stirring constantly, until sugar dissolves. If sugar crystals form on sides of pan, wipe them off. Reduce heat and cook without stirring to the firm ball stage (248°).

Just before syrup reaches 248°, beat egg whites until stiff, but not dry. Gradually pour about half of the cooked syrup in a fine stream over egg whites, beating constantly with electric mixer on medium speed.

Continue to cook remaining syrup to the soft crack stage (272°). Add this syrup, a tablespoonful at a time, to egg white mixture, beating well after each addition with electric mixer or wooden spoon. Continue beating until candy starts to lose its gloss and drops from a spoon in soft peaks.

Stir in vanilla. Pour into lightly buttered 8″ square pan. When cool and firm, cut in 36 pieces. Makes 1½ pounds.

## Variation

**Red Hot Coconut Divinity** Add 1 (3½ oz.) can flaked coconut with vanilla to Red Hot Divinity.

## SEA FOAM

*Sea foams, half-sisters of divinity, are a bit harder, but luscious—
Grandma liked the name and the candy*

| | |
|---|---|
| 1¾ c. light brown sugar | ¼ tsp. salt |
| ¾ c. white sugar | 2 egg whites |
| ½ c. hot water | 1 tsp. vanilla |
| ¼ c. light corn syrup | ½ c. broken walnuts (optional) |

Combine sugars, water, corn syrup and salt in 2-qt. heavy sauce-pan. Cook, stirring constantly, until sugars dissolve and mixture reaches a boil. If sugar crystals form on sides of pan, wipe them off. Continue cooking, without stirring, at a fairly low boil to the hard ball stage (260°). Remove from heat.

At once beat egg whites until stiff. Pour hot syrup in thin stream over egg whites, beating constantly with electric mixer on high speed. Add vanilla; continue beating until candy forms soft peaks and starts to lose its gloss (this will take about 10 minutes).

Stir in nuts. Drop rounded teaspoonfuls onto waxed paper, swirling candy to make peaks. Makes 30 to 36 pieces, or about 1 pound.

## FRUITED SEA FOAM

*Mixed fruits sparkle in snowy candy*

| | |
|---|---|
| 3 c. sugar | ⅛ tsp. salt |
| ⅔ c. water | ½ tsp. vanilla |
| ½ c. light corn syrup | 1 c. candied mixed fruits |
| 2 egg whites | |

Combine sugar, water and syrup in a 2-qt. heavy saucepan. Cook, stirring constantly, until sugar dissolves and mixture reaches a boil. If sugar crystals form on sides of pan, wipe them off. Boil to the hard ball stage (252°).

Combine egg whites and salt, beat until stiff. Pour hot syrup over egg whites, beating constantly until mixture loses gloss.

Add vanilla and beat until mixture forms peaks. Fold in candied mixed fruit, reserving 2 tblsp. for topping. Pour into buttered 8″ square pan. Scatter reserved mixed fruit on top. When cool and firm, cut in squares. Makes about 36 pieces or 1½ pounds.

## NO-COOK DIVINITY

*Pretty, airy and fast to make*

1 (6.5 oz.) pkg. fluffy white
    frosting mix
⅓ c. light corn syrup
1 tsp. vanilla

½ c. boiling water
1 lb. confectioners sugar
Food color (optional)
⅓ c. pecan halves (60)

Combine frosting mix, corn syrup, vanilla and boiling water in small size bowl of electric mixer; beat on high speed until stiff peaks form.

Transfer to large mixing bowl and beat on low speed, gradually adding confectioners sugar. Add food color if desired.

Drop by teaspoonfuls onto waxed paper. At once top each piece with a pecan half. Allow to dry 12 hours or overnight. Makes 60 pieces.

# Elegant American-Style Nougat

Nougat is the aristocratic, world-famous cousin of divinity. The Utah homemaker-home economist who contributed our recipe for the American-style candy says: "This nougat is so delicious that I have to hide it from myself after I've made it!"

It's truly delectable, even though the recipe eliminates some of the frills professional candy makers employ. For instance, classic nougat has very thin Japanese rice wafers on top and bottom. And it always contains honey, almonds (which have been blanched, shredded and toasted) and chopped pistachio nuts.

In our recipe corn syrup ably takes the honey role, and we omit the pistachio nuts. If you're making the candy for Christmas gift boxes or a holiday party, you may want to splurge a little by substituting 1 c. pistachio nuts for 1 c. of the almonds. Pistachios add a pretty touch of green and give an exotic flavor.

Even though American-Style Nougat is a simplified recipe, it still involves work—but is worth it. And you need to eliminate guesswork by using a candy thermometer. You can spread the work over two days if more convenient. Make Part 1 a day or several days ahead, cover it well with waxed paper and store in a cool place. It will be ready when it's time to pour Part 2.

Turn the block of firm candy onto a cutting board or surface and cut it with a sharp knife. The traditional shape of the pieces is rectangular and the size is about 1½" long, ½" wide and about ¾" thick. But we cut the candy in 1" squares. Wrap each piece in waxed paper immediately because the candy may become sticky if exposed to the air. Our recipe-testers cut 4½ ×4" rectangles of waxed paper for each piece and twisted the two ends.

Nougat has splendid keeping qualities when well wrapped and stored in the refrigerator or freezer. You can make it days ahead of Christmas for a holiday treat. Once you do, it's a candy you'll make every year when you start to think about Christmas trees and holly wreaths.

## AMERICAN-STYLE NOUGAT

*The only thing more delicious than a piece of nougat is two pieces!*

*Part 1:*

| | |
|---|---|
| 1½ c. sugar | ¼ c. water |
| 1¼ c. light corn syrup | 3 small egg whites |

*Part 2:*

| | |
|---|---|
| 3 c. sugar | 1 tsp. salt |
| 3 c. light corn syrup | 3 c. blanched, delicately |
| 4 tsp. vanilla | toasted and slivered almonds |
| ½ c. melted butter | |

To make Part 1, combine sugar, corn syrup and water in a 3-qt. heavy saucepan. Cook over medium heat, stirring until sugar dissolves. Continue to cook at a low boil to the soft ball stage on candy thermometer (238°).

When syrup reaches 230°, beat egg whites until they stand in peaks.

When syrup reaches 238°, add it in a fine stream to egg whites, beating constantly with electric mixer on medium speed, or with a wooden spoon, until mixture becomes thick and is lukewarm. It will keep several days if well covered with waxed paper and stored in the refrigerator.

To make Part 2, combine sugar and corn syrup in 4-qt. heavy

saucepan. Cook over medium heat, stirring constantly, to the soft crack stage (275°).

Meanwhile, place Part 1 in lightly buttered large bowl. Pour hot candy (Part 2) over it all at one time. Mix with heavy wooden spoon. Slowly add vanilla and butter, continuing to mix with heavy wooden spoon.

Add salt and nuts, mix again. Turn into 2 well-buttered 9″ square pans, flattening top of candy with buttered hands. Let stand several hours.

Turn onto cutting board and cut each pan of candy into 81 squares, or the desired number of pieces, and wrap with waxed paper. Makes about 5 pounds.

# Dipping Chocolates for Christmas

If you could bring together an exhibit of all the different chocolates hand-dipped in country kitchens at Christmas time, you'd see a breathtaking display. It would rival the showcases of fancy chocolates ($3 to $5 a pound) that tempt visitors into the glittering, exclusive candy shops along holiday-decorated streets in New York, Paris, London and Vienna.

None of the women who make these luscious treats denies it takes time and practice to turn out perfect chocolates. But not one of them says she does not enjoy her annual candy making spree! "My family is so appreciative," they tell you. And someone will add: "We've never found a gift for friends that pleases as much as our homemade candies dipped in chocolate."

The idea of dipping chocolates not only fascinates many homemakers, it also challenges them. A West Coast County Extension Home Economist says the women she works with repeatedly told her they wanted to learn to do it. Their interest prompted her to acquire the necessary knowledge and skills. She's now a champion in her own right and has taught many women to excel in this cookery art.

A Utah homemaker, who is an expert in chocolate dipping, says: "Christmas chocolates are as traditional at our house as the Christmas tree and Santa Claus. We find making the candies is a lot of work but that it is fun if we do it before the Thanksgiving-Christmas rush starts. The entire family gets involved. We have such a feeling of satisfaction when we get the chocolates boxed and stored in a cool place [55 to 60°], ready to give and eat during the holidays."

Besides giving family and friends so much eating pleasure, homemade chocolates sell remarkably well at bazaars and food sales. Be sure to ask a premium price for them. Fresh hand-dipped candies are worth it!

Many mothers make candy dipping a family project. Even if the men do not dip chocolates (a few of them do), they help in other ways. Just ask about the number of dipping forks they've fashioned from wire.

Candy dippers are individualists. A woman who takes up dipping chocolates as a hobby or as her specialty may start out following someone else's directions. But soon she evolves her own techniques and short cuts. Such discoveries are part of the fascination—and the challenge. Two neighbors may even disagree on which ingredients give the best results. But one thing they have in common is pleasure in sharing their chocolates with others.

## KINDS OF CHOCOLATE FOR DIPPING

There are three kinds of chocolate you can use:

*Dipping:* It comes in large chunks and you buy it by the pound from candy stores and supply houses, in some supermarkets (especially as the holiday season approaches) and at candy counters in variety stores once known as dime stores. Many women find dipping chocolate less expensive than semisweet (see below), especially when they dip several pounds of candy. They say it's easy to manage, and they like the results this chocolate gives them.

*Semisweet:* This chocolate comes in 8-ounce packages and is available in practically every food store. While it is more expensive, many find it more convenient when they dip only a pound or two of candy.

*Chocolate Confection Coatings:* Although these coatings look like chocolate, they are a blend of such ingredients as sugar, hard vegetable shortening, cocoa, chocolate flavoring, salt and vanilla. They are marketed by the pound in both dark and milk chocolate flavors and are less sensitive to heat and easier to use. Candy makers consider them an especially good choice for summer use. They are unevenly distributed, but you find them in candy supply stores, in some supermarkets from Thanksgiving to Christmas and in catalogues of reliable mail order houses. Melted confection coating is ready for dipping when it's cooled to 95°.

Confection coatings also come in ivory, delicate pink and pastel green colorings and in butterscotch flavor. It's with these coatings that you sometimes make bark candies.

In our testing, we were enthusiastic about this tip from an Oregon Extension Home Economist. She blends some of the chocolates to make a special coating for exceptionally sweet centers, such as some of the coconut centers. We found that her mixture of ½ dipping chocolate melted with ¼ semisweet and ¼ milk chocolate gives excellent results.

Here is the method we recommend as a good one to follow when you decide to try dipping chocolates:

## HOW TO DIP CHOCOLATES

*Where to Dip:* Work in a cool room, 60 to 65°, and never more than 70°. If you need to cool the room, turn off the heat in advance. If you open a window, lower it a few inches from the top to avoid a draft. Drafts and steam from cooking affect the color and gloss of chocolate. Since too much humidity causes gray streaks in chocolate, try to do the dipping on a dry day.

*Assemble Utensils and Tools:* Include a good candy thermometer. Use it, for temperature is very important, but first test thermometer for accuracy and your altitude (see Index, Candy Thermometer). Since it is sometimes difficult to read a candy thermometer immersed in chocolate, a dough thermometer that registers 70 to 120° often is a good investment.

*Organize Working Area:* If you are right-handed, place surface for candy centers, or whatever you are going to dip, on your left. On your right, provide a surface covered with waxed paper on which to place the dipped candies. For a small amount of candy, wire racks covered with waxed paper are fine. (When they dip larger quantities, some homemakers find a dining table leaf, covered with waxed paper, most convenient. It is easily moved.)

*Get Centers Ready:* They need to be shaped and at room temperature—the temperature of the room in which you will do the dipping. If centers are too cold, as they would be if taken directly from the refrigerator, the finished chocolates will have gray streaks. If centers are too warm, they will be too soft to dip neatly. When you shape them, remember that the chocolate coating will increase their size.

*Prepare the Chocolate:* Grate chocolate or cut it in fine pieces. The amount to use is approximate. One pound will dip about 3 pounds of chocolates with cream centers (fondant) or from 60 to 72 pieces—20 to 24 good-size pieces make about 1 pound. Nougat, jellies, caramels, nuts, dates and raisins take more chocolate. One pound will coat about 2 pounds of them.

*Melt Chocolate:* Put 2 to 3 pounds grated or cut-up chocolate into the top of a double boiler. (If your double boiler is large enough and you wish to dip many candies, increase the amount of chocolate.) Pour boiling water into the bottom of the double boiler and set the top containing chocolate over the bottom containing the water (it will be just below boiling point). Do not let upper part of double boiler touch hot water in lower part. *Use care not to let even one drop of water fall into the chocolate, for it will spoil the entire batch.* Stir the chocolate over hot water constantly with a circular motion to melt it evenly and to avoid overheating it. When chocolate is melted, insert the thermometer; be sure the bulb is immersed in the chocolate. Continue stirring until temperature reaches 120°. Now take top of double boiler out of the hot water and continue stirring chocolate until temperature cools to 70°. The ideal temperature for dipping is 67 to 68°.

*Dip Centers:* Drop a center into chocolate with your left hand. With a dipping fork (directions follow for "How to Make Dipping Forks") in your right hand, gently stir to cover candy completely with chocolate. Slip fork under candy and lift it out quickly. Rap fork two or three times on the rim of the double boiler to remove excess chocolate. If you fail to do this, the base of your candies will have chocolate "skirts," sometimes called "feet." If chocolate gets too cool and thick for dipping, set the top of double boiler over warm water in lower part and stir until it warms enough to continue dipping. (Do not put over heat.) If there is only a small quantity of chocolate, instead of dipping more centers, drop raisins, peanuts or other nuts into it. Stir to coat and drop from teaspoon onto waxed paper.

*Cool Chocolates:* Drop dipped center from fork upside down onto waxed paper. As you lift dipping fork, a thread of chocolate clings to it. Swirl it over top of candy for a decorative touch. Just after you drop candy onto waxed paper, you can top each piece with a nut or you can sprinkle on a little coconut, finely chopped nuts or tiny colored decorating candies. Let cool in the room in which you are doing the dipping. See that chocolates are not in direct sunlight or drafts; otherwise they will have gray streaks. Do not move them until chocolate is firm. If you do, the candies may leak and become sticky. (Chocolates cool fast in a room with temperature of 55 to 65°.)

*Pack Promptly:* When chocolates are cool, look them over. If there are leaks, patch them with a little melted chocolate on your finger or let the family eat them. Put the chocolates in individual paper candy cups and pack them neatly in candy boxes. Brush tops of candy with a soft brush to give them extra gloss. Cover and set in a cool place (55 to 60° is satisfactory) above freezing temperature. If you want to keep them several weeks instead of several days, wrap boxes of candy in aluminum foil and place in the freezer. When ready to use, let thaw several hours at room temperature *before opening.*

## HOW TO DIP CHERRIES

Chocolate-coated cherries require special treatment. They make elegant eating and deserve the special attention they demand. Buy the small maraschino cherries if you can find them (remember that centers increase in size when dipped). Drain cherries overnight or several hours.

Melt Basic Water Fondant (see Index) in top of double boiler over warm, not boiling water. Start with no more than 1 cup fondant. You can add a little cherry juice to tint fondant and to help melt it to the desired consistency—that of a thick syrup. Put a cherry on a cherry dipping fork (directions for "How to Make Dipping Forks" follow) and dip it into the melted fondant. Coat it completely with the fondant and place on waxed paper. The coating will get firm quickly. When all the cherries are fondant-coated and cool, take them, one by one, in your hand and dip only the bottom of the cherry in chocolate ready for dipping. Return to waxed paper and let chocolate harden. Be sure always to place cherries bottom side down after dipping. Then, using a cherry dipping fork, dip the cherries in chocolate the way you do candy centers. Cool and package like other chocolates. The cherries, as they mellow, form a delightful cordial. For this reason, it is especially important to coat them thoroughly with the fondant and chocolate to prevent leaks and to patch leaks if they appear. Do not let the cherries stand long after they have been dipped in fondant, because they start soon to make the cordial; finish dipping in chocolate as soon as cool.

## HOW TO MAKE DIPPING FORKS

You can buy them, of course, but it's no trick to make dipping forks. Husbands of women who make chocolates frequently design these tools. In our Test Kitchens, we made a dipping fork from a piece of lightweight wire clothes hanger, but other wire would do equally well. Bend the wire to make an oval-shaped loop a little smaller than the bowl of a teaspoon; make the handle a little longer than a teaspoon handle. The husband of a Utah candy maker invented her cherry dipping fork. Since the cherries fall through the loop of a regular dipping fork he made a second one just for cherries, pinching in the oval on each side just enough to support the cherries. The loop looks like a figure 8 that doesn't meet in the middle.

## HOW TO HAND-DIP CHOCOLATES

One of our food editors had the inspiring experience of visiting with two homemakers in Utah who literally hand-dip the exquisite chocolates they make for Christmas. By experimenting with techniques, every woman who dips chocolates learns which method she prefers. We think you'll like to have the directions for hand-dipping, too. Our Utah experts make a real production of it, dipping hundreds of chocolates at a time. Here's how they explain what to do if you want to hand-dip chocolates:

Work in a cool room (55 to 60°). Melt dipping chocolate over hot, not boiling water. Pour it onto a large piece of laminated plastic (kitchen counter Formica). A marble slab may be used but it cools chocolate faster.

Beat the chocolate with your hand until it acquires a satiny sheen, has the consistency of thick syrup and feels cool enough for dipping. (It will feel cool to the hand.) Test it by dipping a candy center or a nut. Then pick up a center with your left hand and drop it into the chocolate you scoop into your right hand. Close your fingers lightly around the center and roll it around to coat the candy completely with chocolate. Rap your hand on the plastic counter to shake off excess chocolate and roll the center to the end of your middle finger. Turn your hand over quickly, to drop the chocolate onto waxed paper. With the string of chocolate that clings to your middle finger, make designs on top of the chocolates. You can use symbols that tell what the centers are: V for vanilla fondant, N for nougat, X for caramel, a swirl for jellies. You can decide on your own code.

## SUGGESTIONS FROM SUCCESSFUL CHOCOLATE MAKERS

The Utah homemakers who shared their recipes, methods and chocolates so graciously with our food editor also gave her many extra tips on making chocolates. See if you don't find these ideas helpful, too:

Make fondant for centers a few weeks before the time you plan to dip. The Utah homemakers begin with Basic Cream and Water Fondants (see Index) and while creaming the fondants, they divide each into 4 portions, adding different flavors and tints to each portion. You can add the different flavors, colors and nuts just before shaping the centers, but it really helps to do this ahead. Store the Basic Cream Fondant in covered glass jars or bowls with tight-fitting lids or in tightly closed plastic bags and place in the refrigerator. Store Basic Water Fondant in tightly closed plastic bags and refrigerate.

Make jellied centers, caramels and nougat several days before you dip them to give them plenty of time to set. You can keep them in a very cold room (but above freezing) or in the refrigerator. Keep jellied centers in the refrigerator until just an hour before dipping, so they won't lose their shape.

When you make fondant to shape and dip later, beat it steadily. Beat it slowly if you wish, but never stop until it is white and creamy. (One of the candy makers says she likes to use a 3″ putty knife rather than a spoon or spatula to beat fondant. Her beating strokes are similar to those you'd use to fold flour into angel food cake batter.)

Take your choice of flavorings to add to fondant for centers— extracts of lemon, banana, orange, rum, pistachio, black walnut, maple and mint are all good choices. Our advisers also use fresh lemon and orange juices with grated peel added to intensify the taste, and pineapple juice. Chocolate Mint Fondant (see Index) is one of their recipes which is especially delicious.

For more variety, press pieces of nougat and caramel together before you dip them. Or wrap a strip of caramel around a Brazil nut.

To make the best use of dipping chocolate, dip fondant centers first, then the cherries (first covered with Basic Water Fondant). Next dip nougats, caramels and jellies. Last of all, dip nuts, raisins or coconut; stir to coat them and drop them in clusters on waxed paper—make the clusters about the same size as your chocolates so they will look well in your gift boxes.

Dipping chocolate needs to be cut up for melting—but it's hard. The easiest tool to use is a sharp chisel. If you're planning to melt a lot of chocolate, cut it up the day before.

Sometimes the string of chocolate that is supposed to cling to the fork (or middle finger, if you hand-dip chocolates) fails to appear. You can mark these chocolates later—just dip your finger in the melted chocolate and trace the designs.

Add variety to your gift boxes by "rough dipping" some centers. Our experts especially recommend this treatment for Cherry/Nut Fondant (see Index). Simply add very finely chopped nuts to melted dipping chocolate and dip centers in it. The chocolate should be a little warmer than plain dipping chocolate.

You can also roll dipped chocolates with fondant centers in cookie coconut for another rough coating. Drop the dipped chocolate from your hand or dipping fork into a small bowl of coconut and sprinkle a little more coconut on top. Then put the candy on waxed paper to cool and set.

# Centers for Dipped Chocolates

We have suggested that you make best use of dipping chocolate if you dip the fondant centers first—then nougats, caramels and jellies in succession. Accordingly, our recipe for Basic Cream Fondant comes first; it can be tinted and flavored to make many different chocolate creams.

Following the fondants, you'll find the nougat, caramel and jellied centers we especially recommend for dipping (for other fondants, nougats, caramels and jellied candies, please check the Index).

And we include some specialties—Candy Hearts and Marshmallow Easter Eggs, which you can decorate for special Valentine's and Easter gifts.

## BASIC CREAM FONDANT

*Best fondant for chocolate creams—the verdict of our taste panel*

| | |
|---|---|
| 4 c. sugar | 2 tblsp. butter |
| ½ c. hot water | 1 tsp. vanilla |
| ⅛ tsp. salt | Chocolate for dipping (see |
| 1½ c. heavy cream | Index) |
| ¼ c. light corn syrup | |

Combine sugar, hot water, salt, heavy cream and corn syrup in 3-qt. heavy saucepan. Place over low heat and stir until sugar dissolves and mixture boils. Cover and cook 3 minutes, then remove cover and continue cooking without stirring to the soft ball stage (240°). If sugar crystals form on sides of pan, wipe them off.

Without scraping saucepan, immediately pour fondant onto moist, cold marble slab, baking sheet or platter. Add butter, but do not stir. Let cool until center of fondant mass is lukewarm. If you use a baking sheet, move its position on counter top occasionally to hasten cooling.

When lukewarm, beat with broad spatula, wooden paddle or putty knife until fondant is white and creamy, using a sweeping motion forward from under edge to center, turning fondant occasionally. Then knead with hands until smooth. Add vanilla and knead until blended into fondant. Wrap in waxed paper and store in tightly covered container in refrigerator. (You can divide fondant and store it in glass fruit jars with tight lids.) Let ripen in refrigerator at least 24 hours, but it keeps several weeks. If it gets too dry, cover with a damp cloth.

When ready to dip fondant in chocolate, divide it in fourths and flatten each portion. To each add small amounts of food color to tint, and shape each in a roll 1" in diameter.

Cut ½" (about) slices from rolls and shape in oblongs, balls, squares, or as desired. If fondant sticks to hands, dust them lightly with confectioners sugar. Place individual pieces on wire racks covered with waxed paper or waxed paper spread on any surface. Let stand in cool room (60 to 65° is ideal) for 4 or 5 hours before dipping. Or cover with waxed paper and let stand overnight. Do not refrigerate centers. Dip them when they are the temperature of the cool room in which you will do the dipping. Makes 54 to 60 centers, or about 2 pounds.

## Variations

Make Basic Cream Fondant, omitting vanilla. Divide in 4 equal parts when creaming candy or when shaping fondant for dipping. Flavor and tint each portion differently to make the following kinds:

**Orange/Coconut Fondant**  Add ½ tsp. fresh orange juice, ¼ c. cookie coconut, ¼ tsp. grated orange peel and 2 drops red and 6 drops yellow food color.

**Lemon/Almond Fondant**  Add ½ tsp. fresh lemon juice, ¼ tsp. grated lemon peel, 3 tblsp. finely chopped almonds and 8 drops yellow food color.

**Vanilla Fondant**  This is the same as Basic Cream Fondant, but you add only ¼ tsp. vanilla instead of 1 tsp. for the full recipe, and add 3 drops almond extract.

**Maple/Nut Fondant**  Add ⅛ tsp. maple flavoring and 3 tblsp. chopped walnuts.

## BASIC WATER FONDANT

*This candy mellows delightfully when you put it in the refrigerator*

| | |
|---|---|
| 2 c. sugar | ¼ tsp. almond extract |
| 2 tblsp. light corn syrup | Chocolate for dipping (see |
| ¾ c. boiling water | Index) |
| ⅛ tsp. salt | |

Combine all ingredients, except almond extract and chocolate, in 2-qt. heavy saucepan and stir over low heat until sugar is dissolved and mixture comes to a boil. Cover and boil 1 minute. Then remove lid and cook to the soft ball stage (238 to 240°). If sugar crystals form on sides of pan, wipe them off.

Pour at once onto a cool, moist baking sheet, platter or marble slab. Let cool until lukewarm.

Work with broad spatula or wooden paddle until fondant is white and creamy. Add almond extract. Knead until smooth. Put in a plastic bag and close tightly. Place in refrigerator to mellow at least 24 hours, or for several weeks.

Divide the fondant into 4 equal portions when getting ready to dip in chocolate or use in other ways. Shape each portion in a roll 1″ in diameter. Then cut off pieces to shape centers as desired. Makes about 1 pound.

N O T E : This is the fondant good candy makers prefer to use when coating maraschino cherries with chocolate (see Dipping Chocolates in Index).

## CHERRY/NUT FONDANT

*Pretty pink fondant coated with the chocolate tastes great. Youngsters especially like the Cherry Bars*

| | |
|---|---|
| 6 tblsp. light corn syrup | 1 tsp. vanilla |
| ¼ c. maraschino cherry juice | 1 c. finely chopped nuts |
| 1¼ c. heavy cream | Chocolate for dipping (see |
| 4 c. sugar | Index) |
| ½ c. chopped maraschino cherries (well drained) | |

Combine corn syrup, cherry juice, cream and sugar in 3-qt. heavy saucepan. Cook over low heat, stirring constantly, until sugar is dissolved and mixture boils. Cover and let mixture boil 3 minutes, watching that it does not boil over. Remove cover, add cherries and cook to the soft ball stage (236°). If sugar crystals form on sides of pan, wipe them off.

Remove from heat; add vanilla and pour onto cool, moist baking sheet, marble slab or platter. Let cool until lukewarm (110°).

Beat until creamy and mixture thickens. Knead until smooth. Add nuts. Wrap in waxed paper and store in covered container in refrigerator at least 24 hours or several days.

When ready to dip in chocolate, remove candy from refrigerator. When it warms enough in room temperature to shape, form 8 flattened mounds of candy. Shape each portion in a roll 1″ in diameter. Slice off ½″ slices and shape in ovals, or as desired for dipping in chocolate. Makes 62 centers, or about 2½ pounds.

## Variations

**Cherry/Coconut Fondant**  Substitute 1 c. cookie coconut for the nuts.

**Cherry Bars**  Omit nuts from Cherry/Nut Fondant. Cut the rolls in 60 pieces; shape each into a bar about 2″ long. Instead of dipping in plain chocolate, add 1 c. very finely chopped nuts to chocolate. Dip candy bars in this. The coating with nuts in it will be rough.

### CHOCOLATE FONDANT

*Dip this fondant in chocolate and watch it disappear at food sales*

| | |
|---|---|
| 3 c. sugar | 2 squares semisweet chocolate |
| ⅛ tsp. salt | 1½ tsp. vanilla |
| ¾ c. heavy cream | Chocolate for dipping (see |
| 6 tblsp. milk | Index) |
| 6 tblsp. light corn syrup | |

Combine sugar, salt, cream, milk, corn syrup and chocolate in 3-qt. heavy saucepan. Cook over low heat, stirring until sugar dissolves and mixture reaches a boil.

Cover and let boil 3 minutes. (Watch that candy does not boil over.) Remove cover and cook, without stirring, to the soft ball stage (238°). If sugar crystals form on sides of pan, wipe them off.

Pour at once onto cool, moist platter, baking sheet or marble slab. Let cool until lukewarm. Then beat until fondant becomes creamy.

Knead with hands until smooth; add vanilla, working it in to mix. Wrap with waxed paper, put in container, cover tightly and store in refrigerator at least 24 hours, or for several weeks.

When ready to coat with chocolate, let candy reach temperature of cool room in which you will do the dipping. Divide in 4 portions and flatten each. Roll each to make a roll 1″ in diameter. Cut ½″ slices and shape in ovals, rounds or as you like. Put in a cool place until set. Then dip in chocolate. Makes about 48 centers or 2 pounds.

NOTE: For a more pronounced chocolate flavor, use 1 square unsweetened and 1 square semisweet chocolate.

## Variations

**Chocolate Mint Fondant Creams** Omit vanilla and add 2 or 3 drops oil of peppermint to Chocolate Fondant.

**Coconut Cream Fondant** Omit chocolate. Mix in 1 c. cookie coconut along with the vanilla. Work to distribute coconut evenly. Shape in balls and place in a cool room to set. Dip in chocolate.

## COCONUT CANDY CENTERS

*Especially for the lovers of coconut and chocolate—simply delicious*

| | |
|---|---|
| 1 c. sugar | ½ tsp. almond extract |
| 1½ c. light corn syrup | 65 to 70 toasted almonds |
| ½ c. water | Chocolate for dipping (see |
| 1 (14 oz.) pkg. flaked coconut | Index) |
| (about 4 c.) | |

Combine sugar, corn syrup and water in 2-qt. heavy saucepan. Cook over low heat, stirring constantly until sugar dissolves. Cook to the soft ball stage (236°). If sugar crystals form on sides of pan, wipe them off.

Remove from heat; add coconut and almond extract. Pour onto marble or laminated plastic counter top and let cool.

When cool, shape into large ball with hands, cover with waxed paper and store in a cold place or in refrigerator overnight, or until ready to dip with chocolate.

When ready to dip, shape coconut candy centers into ovals or balls and put a toasted almond on top of each. Dip in chocolate. Makes 65 to 70 centers, or about 2 pounds before dipping.

## Pioneer Potato Candy

Potato candy is an "I remember" sweet—there was bustling excitement in grandmothers' kitchens when this treat was made for the Christmas holidays. Grandchildren of those days haven't forgotten how wonderful it tasted.

A FARM JOURNAL reader recently wrote from Iowa: "Last year the kids came home from Grandma's with the recipe for potato candy and a sample of it. I hardly could believe you could make such wonderful candy with potatoes. I tried the recipe and had success with it."

A West Virginia homemaker echoes her sentiments: "My family likes potato candy very much. Whenever we make it, we remember the handed-down story about the first time my mother made it. She began by cooking and mashing a very large potato. Before the candy making ended, we added 5 pounds of confectioners sugar. Now it takes the whole family to select just the right size potato to make enough but not too much."

Our recipe for Pioneer Potato Candy, contributed by a Wisconsin homemaker, gives the measurement of cooked, unseasoned, mashed potato. Potatoes have a high water content, which depends on the climate (dry or wet season), the time of year (new potatoes contain more water than old ones), and the variety. The amount of water in the potato affects the quantity of confectioners sugar you need to add.

The trick is to add enough sugar to produce a candy mixture with the consistency of a stiff dough so that you can knead it. The result is a type of fondant that you can dip in melted chocolate and roll in chopped nuts or coconut. Or you can omit the dipping and decorate the candy pieces with nuts. This, like all other potato candies, is at its best when eaten fresh.

*GIFT CANDY. When you pack gift boxes, remember that assortments look more exciting. Brighten a box of chocolate fudge with a few Pastel Bonbons, or caramels wrapped in colored foil instead of waxed paper. Make Christmas Ribbons—striped red, green and chocolate. Or bright pink Christmas Cherry Fudge. (See Index for recipes.)*

## PIONEER POTATO CANDY

*This is a big recipe; you may wish to make half of it the first time*

| | |
|---|---|
| 1 c. warm unseasoned mashed potato | 1 lb. chocolate confection coating or chocolate for dipping (see Index) |
| ½ tsp. salt | |
| 2 tsp. vanilla | ⅔ c. ground salted peanuts, or |
| 2 lbs. confectioners sugar | 1 c. shredded coconut |

Combine potato, salt and vanilla in a 4-qt. mixing bowl. Sift confectioners sugar over potato, stirring and adding about 1 c. at a time. Mixture will liquefy when first sugar is added, then gradually begin to thicken. When it becomes the consistency of stiff dough, knead it even though all the sugar has not been added (likewise, add more sugar if needed).

After kneading, cover with a damp cloth; chill until a small spoonful can be rolled into a ball.

Shape in small (½") balls. Dip balls in melted chocolate, then roll in peanuts or coconut. Makes about 8 dozen ½" balls, or 2 pounds.

## ORIENTAL CREAMS

*Shape and dip centers at once for they soften upon standing. They're luscious after candy mellows*

| | |
|---|---|
| 2 c. sugar | 1 tsp. vanilla |
| 1 c. water | 1 egg white, stiffly beaten |
| 1 tblsp. light corn syrup | 1 lb. (about) chocolate for dipping (see Index) |
| ¼ tsp. glycerin | |

Combine sugar, water and corn syrup in 2-qt. heavy saucepan; bring to a boil, stirring constantly until sugar is dissolved. When mixture boils, add glycerin. Reduce heat and cover for 3 minutes. Uncover and cook without stirring to soft ball stage (240°). Remove from heat.

Rinse a large, heatproof platter with water; pour candy mixture onto platter. Cool to lukewarm.

Put vanilla in center of candy; spread beaten egg white over top Beat until the fondant is white.

Knead to remove any lumps. Shape into about 40 balls. Dip immediately in chocolate.

## *Variation*

**Nut Creams**  Roll undipped fondant into small balls and flatten slightly. Spread a little melted chocolate on top and press on a pecan or walnut half. Dip in chocolate.


## FRENCH CREMO

*A luscious version of fondant*

4 c. sugar
2 c. heavy cream
½ tsp. cream of tartar
1 tsp. vanilla

Food color (optional)
1 lb. chocolate confection coating
(see Index)

Combine sugar, cream and cream of tartar in 3-qt. heavy saucepan. Cook over low heat, stirring constantly, until sugar dissolves. Cook to the soft ball stage (236°). Watch carefully to avoid boiling over. If sugar crystals form on sides of pan, wipe them off.

Pour onto buttered baking sheets or platters (do not scrape saucepan); let stand until lukewarm.

Work or cream like fondant until creamy and light in color. Add vanilla and food color to tint delicately, if desired; work in to mix.

Shape in pieces as desired (ovals, rounds, squares, etc.).

Dip in melted chocolate confection coating. Makes 3½ pounds.


**To Make a Variety of Bonbons**  Omit vanilla when making French Cremo. Work and cream as for fondant. Divide in quarters.

To one part add 3 drops green food color and 2 to 3 drops mint extract.

To the second part add 2 tblsp. finely chopped pecans and 2 to 3 drops maple flavoring.

To the third portion add 2 to 3 drops yellow food color and 3 drops lemon extract.

To the remaining part, add ⅛ tsp. vanilla and 2 tblsp. chopped walnuts.

Shape in oval pieces and dip in melted chocolate confection coating. Makes 23 to 25 bonbons, or about 3½ pounds.

## OPERA CREAM CENTERS

*All they need for perfection is a quick dip in chocolate coating*

2 c. sugar
1 c. light cream, scalded (or
    ½ c. heavy cream plus ½ c.
    dairy half-and-half)
1 tblsp. light corn syrup
⅛ tsp. salt

½ tsp. flavoring (vanilla, maple,
    rum or fruit)
¼ c. chopped nuts (optional)
Chocolate for dipping or
    confection coating (see Index)

Combine sugar, ½ c. scalded cream and corn syrup in 2-qt. heavy saucepan. Cook over medium heat to the soft ball stage (238°), stirring constantly until mixture comes to a boil, then stir occasionally. Mixture tends to foam, so be careful not to let it boil over.

When mixture reaches 238°, add remaining half of hot cream slowly, stirring constantly; cook again to 238°. Remove from heat.

Pour at once onto a marble slab or chilled jelly roll pan that has been wiped with a clean damp cloth.

Let mixture stand 3 to 5 minutes, then make several light gashes with a knife (do not cut through to the slab or pan); add salt and flavoring.

As soon as candy can be handled, start working it with a wide spatula or fondant scraper, turning the outside edges over the center; this hastens cooling the center, which is important. Continue until mixture is thick and hard to work. As soon as it is firm and does not stick to the hand, knead with hands until it is creamy, then add nuts, folding them in while kneading.

Place in an airtight container and store in refrigerator until firm.

When candy is firm, shape it in ½″ balls and dip in chocolate. Makes about 48 pieces, or 1½ pounds.

N O T E : Marble has a natural coolness and often is preferred by professional candy makers. It is heavy and does not move around when you work candy on it. After flavoring has been added to candy, you may also add food color, if you wish.

## CREAMY WHITE FUDGE CENTERS

*Candy is actually a light caramel color. It sells fast at bazaars*

4 c. sugar
⅛ tsp. salt
1 c. evaporated milk
¼ c. water
6 tblsp. light corn syrup
¼ c. butter (½ stick)

1 tsp. vanilla
1 c. chopped nuts or candied
cherries
Chocolate for dipping (see
Index)

Combine sugar, salt, evaporated milk, water and corn syrup in 3-qt. heavy saucepan. Bring to a boil over low heat, stirring constantly until mixture reaches a boil. Cover and let boil 3 minutes. Remove cover and cook, stirring occasionally to prevent scorching, to the soft ball stage (236°). If sugar crystals form on sides of pan, wipe them off.

Add butter and immediately pour onto cool buttered baking sheet, marble slab or platter. Let candy cool until lukewarm (110°). Add vanilla.

Beat until candy thickens and loses its gloss. Mix in nuts or candied cherries. Spread into buttered 13×9×2″ pan. Cool until firm, then cut in pieces. Shape each piece in a ball. Dip in chocolate. Makes about 60 centers for dipping, or 2½ pounds.

## TRUFFLES

*Too delicious for words to describe*

1½ lbs. milk chocolate (3 c.
shaved or finely cut and
firmly packed)
⅓ c. heavy cream
⅓ c. dairy half-and-half

1½ tsp. vanilla
Chocolate or white confection
coating, or chocolate for
dipping (see Index)

Melt chocolate in top of double boiler over hot (not boiling) water. When melted, beat until smooth.

Meanwhile, combine heavy cream and half-and-half in a small saucepan; heat to scalding. Remove from heat and let stand until temperature is about 130°.

Add warm cream to melted chocolate all at once. Beat until

smooth and well blended. Remove from heat; add vanilla and let cool.

When cool, beat with electric mixer until candy is light and rather fluffy. Let stand in refrigerator until firm.

When firm, roll a teaspoonful of candy into a ball in palms of hands. Roll each ball immediately in chocolate coating. Makes about 36 to 40 truffles, or 2 pounds.

N O T E : The balls of candy may also be rolled in chocolate shot (jimmies) or in cinnamon-flavored cocoa, made by sifting together ¼ c. cocoa and 1 tblsp. cinnamon.

## NOUGAT CENTERS

*Chocolate-covered candy says "Merry Christmas" in a sweet way*

2 c. sugar
1½ c. light corn syrup
1 c. water
2 egg whites
3 tblsp. honey
½ c. finely chopped cashew nuts
  or almonds

½ c. finely chopped candied
  cherries
Chocolate for dipping (see
  Index)

Combine sugar, corn syrup and water in 2-qt. heavy saucepan. Cook over medium heat, stirring constantly, until sugar dissolves. Then cook to the soft crack stage (285°).

Meanwhile, beat egg whites until peaks form; fold in honey.

Pour hot syrup in a fine stream into egg whites, beating constantly with electric mixer on medium speed until mixture thickens and loses its gloss.

Stir in nuts and cherries, mixing well.

Pour into 2 buttered 8″ square pans. When cool, cover and place in refrigerator or cool place (55 to 60°). Let stand a few days before dipping in chocolate.

When ready to dip, cut candy in each pan in 8 strips and then remove from pans. Cut in pieces with scissors. Shape in squares, ovals or as you wish. Dip in chocolate. Makes 128 (1″) squares (64 pieces per pan).

# Caramels Supreme

What a hard choice for candy lovers! Whether to eat these superior caramels as soon as they're firm—or hold them for a chocolate coating. You can enjoy them both ways if you follow our directions. Pour half the batch into a jelly roll pan and store it, uncut, in the refrigerator or cool place for two or three days, until it's set and you're ready to dip. Pour the other half into a square pan, to cut when firm. Wrap pieces in waxed paper as soon after cutting as possible or they'll be sticky.

There's no law against dipping all the caramels. Nor do you have to dip any of them, but if you don't you'll miss one of the candy kitchen's best gifts. You can't beat the chocolate-caramel combination.

It takes a long time to cook caramels, up to 3 hours. Be sure you have the time you need before you start.

## CARAMELS SUPREME

*Our first choice of caramels to dip in chocolate—also good plain*

4 c. sugar
2 c. light corn syrup
½ tsp. salt
4 c. heavy cream
1 (14½ oz.) can evaporated milk (1⅔ c.)
1 square semisweet chocolate

1 square unsweetened chocolate
1 tblsp. vanilla
1 c. finely chopped nuts (optional)
Chocolate confection coating or chocolate for dipping (see Index)

Combine sugar, corn syrup, salt and 2 c. cream in 6-qt. heavy saucepan. Bring to a boil, stirring constantly until sugar is dissolved. Slowly add remaining 2 c. cream, stirring constantly. When mixture reaches the soft ball stage (232°), slowly pour in the evaporated milk, making sure the candy mixture never stops boiling. Stir gently while you add the evaporated milk. Add the chocolates; cook to the firm ball stage (248°).

Remove from heat. Add vanilla and nuts. Pour half of candy into buttered 8″ square pan; pour the other half into buttered 15½ × 10½ × 1″ jelly roll pan.

When cool and firm, cover candy in jelly roll pan with foil and place in refrigerator. Use this for dipping in chocolate.

Cut candy in 8″ square pan in 1″ squares when firm; you'll have 64 pieces. If you are not going to serve candy promptly, wrap each caramel in waxed paper.

Let candy in jelly roll pan set 2 or 3 days before dipping it in chocolate. On dipping day, move it from the refrigerator to the cool room in which you will do the dipping. Cut it in 50 pieces—form in squares, oblongs or any desired shape. Place on waxed paper and let stand 1 hour, or until it reaches room temperature. Then dip in chocolate. Recipe makes 3½ pounds caramels, before dipping.

## Variations

**Caramel/Brazil Nut Chocolates**   Wrap 1 piece of Caramels Supreme around a Brazil nut. Repeat with as many nuts as desired. Dip in chocolate.

**Caramel/Nougat Chocolates**   Press half pieces of Nougat Centers (see Index) and Caramels Supreme together; shape as desired and dip in chocolate.

**Snappers**   Omit nuts from Caramels Supreme. Arrange groups of 3 or 4 cashew nuts or pecan halves on buttered baking sheets 2″ apart to make clusters. When Caramels Supreme are cooked and just after removing from heat, drop 1 tsp. hot candy over each cluster of nuts to form turtles (snappers). You can shape them a little when they are cool. Or if you prefer, press a caramel, when cool enough to handle, on each nut cluster and shape. Let part of the nuts show, regardless of which way you make the snappers. Spread tops with melted chocolate, or dip in chocolate. Half of the recipe for Caramels Supreme makes about 150 Snappers.

## JELLIED CENTERS

*Fruit-flavored candies contrast prettily with their chocolate coats*

| | |
|---|---|
| 2 c. sugar | 1 drop red food color |
| 3 tblsp. unflavored gelatin | 4 drops yellow food color |
| 1 c. pineapple juice or water | 1 c. finely chopped nuts |
| Juice and finely grated peel of | (optional) |
|   1 lemon | Chocolate for dipping (see |
| Juice and finely grated peel of |   Index) |
|   1 orange | |

Combine sugar and gelatin in 2-qt. heavy saucepan; mix well.

Heat pineapple juice to a boil; add to gelatin-sugar mixture and stir until gelatin is dissolved. Bring to a boil; lower heat and simmer steadily 20 minutes.

Remove from heat; add lemon and orange juices and peel; stir in food color and nuts. Let stand a few minutes, then strain into 2 buttered 9×5×3″ loaf pans. Candy should be from ½ to 1″ thick in pans. Cover and refrigerate 24 hours, or until firm.

An hour before you are ready to dip jellied candy, remove it from refrigerator to a cool room (55 to 60°). Cut in pieces about 1¼ × 1″, or shape as desired; place on waxed paper dusted with cornstarch (this prevents sticking while candies wait to be dipped). Dip in chocolate. Makes 72 pieces.

NOTE: You can divide candy in half and tint one part red and one part green for Christmas.

## Variation

**Plain Jellied Candy**  Cut firm jellied mixture in 1″ strips crosswise and pull from pan. Candy will seem somewhat rubbery. Roll each strip in sifted confectioners sugar, then cut each strip in pieces, rolling them in confectioners sugar to coat thoroughly.

## MARSHMALLOW EASTER EGGS

*A baker's dozen of the prettiest and tastiest chocolate-coated eggs ever to come from country kitchens*

| | |
|---|---|
| 2 envelopes unflavored gelatin | Flour |
| 2 tblsp. cold water | ¾ lb. chocolate for dipping or |
| ½ c. boiling water | chocolate confection coating, |
| 2 c. sugar | melted (see Index) |
| ½ tsp. salt | Regal Icing |
| ½ tsp. vanilla | |

Put gelatin in top of double boiler; add cold water. When gelatin softens, add boiling water and stir well. Add sugar and salt. Put over boiling water and stir until sugar dissolves completely.

Pour into large bowl of electric mixer and beat at high speed until mixture is thick but not as stiff as beaten egg whites. Add vanilla.

Meanwhile, spread flour 2″ deep in a large pan. Push an egg

(in shell) into the flour at intervals, making hollow spaces in which to mold the marshmallow mixture.

Drop marshmallow mixture into the flour molds. Sprinkle flour lightly over top and put in cold place until set. Remove mixture from one mold and you have a half-egg. Trim the flat side of marshmallow half-egg to make it even. You can dip it in melted chocolate to cover and decorate with Regal Icing.

Or you can put two halves together to make an egg, as follows: Dip the rounded part of a half-egg in melted chocolate; set aside to cool, flat (uncoated) side down. Trim flat side of second half-egg (to make it even), lift from mold and completely coat with chocolate. Quickly press its flat side against the flat side of the cooled half-egg and you have a whole egg. The chocolate will hold it together.

When chocolate-coated eggs are cool, trim with Regal Icing put through cake decorator tube. Make ruffles around them to cover seam where the two halves join and to provide decoration. Write names of children on their eggs with the icing, or decorate with tiny designs pressed through fine tips of a cake decorator tube. Frosting may be left white or tinted in pastel colors. Makes 13 eggs (or 26 half-eggs).


## REGAL ICING

*Pure white and so decorative on chocolate-coated Easter eggs*

3 egg whites                          Sifted confectioners sugar
½ tsp. cream of tartar

Beat egg whites with cream of tartar until frothy. Gradually add confectioners sugar until mixture is thick enough to hold its shape, but not so stiff that it won't pass through a cake decorator tube. Test it this way: Cut through icing with a knife. If the line remains, it is stiff enough. As you decorate eggs, if icing becomes too stiff mix in a little lemon juice to moisten. Makes enough icing to decorate 13 Marshmallow Easter Eggs.

NOTE: When not in use, keep icing covered with a damp cloth so that it does not dry out.

## CANDY HEARTS

*Hearts and flowers for Valentine's Day—hearts are pink divinity dipped in chocolate or white coating and decorated with icing*

4 c. sugar
1 c. light corn syrup
2 c. water
2 tsp. vanilla
4 drops peppermint extract
10 drops red food color

2 large egg whites, stiffly beaten
Chocolate or white confection
coating or chocolate for
dipping (see Index)
Ornamental Icing

Combine sugar, corn syrup and water in 3-qt. heavy saucepan; cook, stirring, until sugar is dissolved. Continue to cook to the hard ball stage (258°). If any sugar crystals form on sides of pan during cooking, wipe them off. Add vanilla, peppermint extract and food color.

Pour slowly onto beaten egg whites, beating constantly until candy begins to set and can be molded with hands. (Do not let it get too firm or it will be more difficult to handle.)

Divide in half. Lift one half to waxed paper spread on counter and roll with rolling pin to make an oblong ½" thick. Repeat with other half.

Cut with a heart-shaped cookie cutter (2¼" wide in largest place). With the point of a paring knife, cut out the dip in the heart to give candy a better heart shape. Reroll scraps and cut in hearts until all candy mixture is used. Let stand on waxed paper several hours, or until dry. Place in covered containers with waxed paper between layers for a few days until you are ready to dip and decorate hearts.

Dip candy hearts in melted confection coating or dipping chocolate. Cool on waxed paper.

Divide and tint Ornamental Icing with food colors as desired. Put through decorating tube with flower tips. Let flowers dry on waxed paper. Then put a little icing on the bottom of each flower (to hold it in place) and arrange on candy hearts. Makes 32 hearts about 2½" wide when dipped with confection coating or dipping chocolate.

**Ornamental Icing** In a small glass mixing bowl, beat together 2 small egg whites (room temperature), 2 c. confectioners sugar, sifted, and ½ tsp. cream of tartar. Beat until icing stands in peaks, about 10 minutes. Use as directed to decorate Candy Hearts. Keep icing covered with a damp cloth when not in use, so it does not dry out. Makes enough icing to decorate 32 Candy Hearts.

## BRITTLE BUTTER CRUNCH

*Top these with nuts, if you wish, after you dip them*

½ c. butter
½ c. white sugar
3 tblsp. brown sugar
1 tblsp. light corn syrup
1 tblsp. water

¼ tsp. baking soda
1 tsp. vanilla
½ lb. chocolate for dipping (see Index)

Melt butter in 2-qt. heavy saucepan; add sugars, corn syrup and water. Bring to boil, stirring constantly, and cook to soft crack stage (290°). Remove from heat; stir in baking soda and vanilla.

Pour into buttered 8″ square pan. Allow to set 3 minutes. Mark the candy with a knife into 36 squares; when cool and firm, cut.

When pieces are brittle, dip in melted chocolate. Makes 36 pieces.

## RAISIN/NUT CHOCOLATE STICKS

*Pour out luscious caramel thick with raisins and nuts; cut in sticks and dip them in melted chocolate*

1 c. brown sugar, firmly packed
1 c. light corn syrup
1½ tsp. salt
1⅓ c. light cream
3 c. seedless raisins

1 c. chopped walnuts
1½ tsp. vanilla
1½ lbs. chocolate confection coating or chocolate for dipping (see Index)

Combine sugar, corn syrup, salt and cream in 2-qt. heavy saucepan. Cook over medium heat, stirring constantly until sugar is dissolved. Then cook, stirring occasionally to prevent sticking, to the firm ball stage (246 to 248°). Remove from heat.

Add raisins, nuts and vanilla. Mix well and pour into 9″ square pan that has been buttered then dusted with cornstarch. Cool several hours or overnight.

Cut in 44 slender bars or sticks and dip in melted chocolate confection coating or in dipping chocolate. Place on waxed paper to cool. Makes 3½ pounds.

# Fondant Delicacies

Fondant is a foundation candy. From it you build many tempting candies and confections that aren't identified as fondant. Chocolate creams with fondant centers are one luscious example. Mints in pretty, soft colors show up at supper parties and receptions—they're pure fondant. The candy also deliciously stuffs big, plump prunes and dates. And made into satiny coating, it covers almonds, raisins and many candy centers with beauty and marvelous flavor.

Some candy makers, failing to recognize what they can do with fondant, park their imaginations when working with it. Recipes for exciting fondant treats follow. Use them and the candy's popularity will skyrocket at your house. The first step, though, is to make fine-textured, creamy candy free from noticeable sugar crystals. Here's the way to do it:

Put candy mixture over low heat and cook, stirring constantly until sugar dissolves and mixture comes to a boil. Cover saucepan for 3 minutes while the candy continues boiling. Remove cover and cook without stirring at a steady, fairly low boil to the soft ball stage (238 to 240°).

Throughout cooking, keep sugar crystals wiped from sides of saucepan with damp, cloth-covered table fork or pastry brush.

Remove cooked candy from heat and pour at once, without scraping pan, onto a cooled, slightly damp baking sheet, platter or marble slab. A good way to cool the surface is to cover it with cracked ice. Wipe off ice and excess moisture just before pouring candy. Pour candy about ¼" thick.

*CANDY FOR THE HOLIDAYS—"Stained glass" hanging ornaments are hard candy poured free-form or into foil molds (directions, page 161). On tray: Honeyed Popcorn, page 198, Apricot Nuggets, page 186, Peanut Butter Fudge, page 28, and sliced Holiday Logs, page 145.*

Cool until lukewarm, judging temperature at center of candy mass with your hand.

Work with broad spatula or wooden paddle (you can buy these). Push the spatula under the edge of fondant and use a sweeping motion to the center and then back over to the edge. Turn candy frequently while working it. Work (beat) it until fondant turns white and becomes creamy.

Knead until smooth, giving special attention to any hard spots.

Add vanilla or other flavoring and food color if desired. Mix it in thoroughly. (If you wish, divide fondant in portions and flavor and tint parts separately. Then wrap and store in separate containers.) Or you can flavor and tint it when you're ready to use.

Wrap in waxed paper, put in a jar or bowl, cover tightly and store in refrigerator. Let mellow at least 48 hours or for several days or weeks. If fondant starts to dry out, cover with damp cloth.

## CREAMY FONDANT

*It's what you create with fondant that brings extravagant praises*

| | |
|---|---|
| 2 c. sugar | ½ c. water |
| ⅓ c. light corn syrup | ⅛ tsp. cream of tartar |

Combine all ingredients in 2-qt. heavy saucepan. Cook over medium heat, stirring constantly until sugar dissolves and mixture comes to a boil. Cover saucepan for 3 minutes; remove cover and cook without stirring to the soft ball stage (240°). If sugar crystals form on sides of pan, wipe them off.

Remove from heat. Pour at once onto a cold, slightly wet platter or baking sheet. Cool until center of candy feels lukewarm.

Beat with spatula until white and creamy. Then knead with hands until smooth. Shape into a soft ball. Store in covered dish in refrigerator for at least 2 or 3 days before using. Makes 1 pound.

When ready to use, divide candy in 2 or 4 parts if you wish to make different kinds of candies or confections with the fondant.

Melt fondant over hot (175°), not boiling, water. Here are treats to make with it:

**Autumn Candy Wafers** To ¼ Creamy Fondant, melted, add 2 drops yellow food color and 4 drops lemon extract. Stir gently just to blend. Drop from teaspoon onto waxed paper to make 18 round wafers.

**Fondant-stuffed Dates**  To ¼ Creamy Fondant, melted, add 1 drop red food color to make a luscious pink and 2 drops vanilla. Stir gently just to blend. Remove from heat. Cool slightly. Stuff into 24 moist, pitted dates. Roll dates in 1 tblsp. confectioners sugar.

**Nut Creams**  To ¼ Creamy Fondant, melted, add 1 drop green food color and 2 drops vanilla. Stir gently just to blend. Remove from heat. Cool until firm enough to handle. Form into small balls with hands. Balls should be ½″ in diameter. Press each ball between 2 pecan halves. Makes 30 to 31 candies.

**Fondant Kisses**  To ¼ Creamy Fondant, melted, add ¼ c. finely chopped nuts and a few drops of vanilla. Stir gently just to blend. Remove from heat and cool slightly. Drop from teaspoon onto waxed paper to form small mounds. Shape mounds with fingers to give them peaks. Serve as is, or dip lower half of kisses in melted dipping chocolate or confection coating (see Index). Or dip entire kiss in the chocolate coating. A good way to do this is to insert a toothpick through the peak of each kiss, dip candy in chocolate and then stand it, peak side down, with end of pick inserted in Styrofoam until chocolate is firm. Repeat with all candies. Cooling the kisses on the wooden picks gives them an attractive chocolate peak. When chocolate is firm, remove picks. Makes 20 to 21 kisses.

## FAST-COOK FONDANT

*Confectioners sugar sweetens fondant, easy to make and shape*

| | |
|---|---|
| 1 lb. confectioners sugar, sifted | ½ c. light corn syrup |
| ⅓ c. butter or margarine | 1 tsp. vanilla |

Combine half of confectioners sugar, butter and corn syrup in 3-qt. heavy saucepan. Cook over low heat, stirring constantly, until mixture comes to a full boil. Quickly stir in remaining confectioners sugar and vanilla. Remove from heat.

Stir only until mixture holds its shape. Pour into buttered 8 or 9″ square pan. Cool just enough to handle.

Knead until smooth. (If fondant gets too hard to knead, work it with a spoon to soften and then knead.) If you want to make different candies, divide into 2 or 4 parts. Knead in food colors and flavorings as desired. Makes about 1½ pounds.

## Variations

**Fast-Cook Chocolate Fondant**  Sift ¼ c. cocoa with 1 lb. confectioners sugar. Then proceed as for Fast-Cook Fondant. Delicious for Fondant-stuffed Prunes.

You can divide Fast-Cook Fondant in 4 equal parts and with one part make each of the following:

**Fondant-stuffed Prunes**  Stuff fondant into 30 pitted prunes (one 12 oz. pkg.). Tuck a walnut piece into each prune alongside the fondant. You will need about ¼ c. walnut pieces. Coat prunes completely with dipping chocolate or chocolate confection coating (see Index), if desired.

**Mint Patties**  Knead 1 drop green food color and 2 drops peppermint extract into one part Fast-Cook Fondant. Shape in 15 balls of equal size. Flatten with hands to make patties. Press top of candy mints with fork having 3 or 4 tines to make decorative top. Or knead 1 or 2 drops oil of cinnamon, peppermint or cloves and your choice of other food colors into fondant instead of peppermint extract and green food color.

**Fondant Bonbons**  Knead ¼ tsp. almond extract into one part Fast-Cook Fondant. Shape in 20 balls of equal size with walnuts in center. You will need 3 tblsp. walnut pieces. Roll balls in 1 tblsp. red or green colored sugar and then in 1 tblsp. multicolored candy sprinkles.

**Miniature Fondant Eggs**  Knead ¼ tsp. almond extract and 2 drops blue food color and 1 drop green food color into one part Fast-Cook Fondant to make it a robin's egg blue. (Leave some of fondant white for candy eggs if you wish.) Shape fondant with hands into 162 tiny eggs. Lay on waxed paper. Decorate eggs with brown food color made by combining 2 drops red, 1 drop blue and 1 drop yellow food color. Dip a small clean paint brush with fairly stiff bristles into brown food color; push bristles with your thumb over candy eggs to speckle them with brown. Serve 3 eggs in each Tiny Coconut Cookie (recipe follows).

## TINY COCONUT COOKIES

*These two-bite confections hold tiny candy eggs of robin's egg blue*

½ c. soft butter, or ¼ c.
   butter and ¼ c. shortening
¼ c. brown sugar, firmly packed
1 egg yolk
½ tsp. vanilla
1 c. sifted flour

¼ tsp. salt
1 egg white, slightly beaten
1¼ c. cookie coconut
Miniature Fondant Eggs (see
   preceding recipe)

Combine butter, sugar, egg yolk and vanilla in mixing bowl. Mix thoroughly.

Combine flour and salt and stir to mix. Add to first mixture. Blend well.

Roll dough, 1 tsp. at a time, into a ball and then dip in egg white. (Use 2 egg whites, if necessary.) Roll balls in coconut to coat.

Place 1" apart on ungreased baking sheet. Press thumb gently into center of each ball to make indentation. (The cookies when baked will hold fondant eggs.)

Bake in preheated moderate oven (350°) 10 to 12 minutes. Remove from baking sheet. Cool on wire racks.

At serving time, place 3 Miniature Fondant Eggs in the indentation in each cookie. Or if you prefer, you can make the candy eggs a little larger and put only 1 egg in each cookie. Eggs may be made ahead and stored in airtight containers, set in a cool place. Makes 54 cookies.

N O T E : To secure the Fondant Eggs in place, you can fasten them to the cookies with dabs of Royal Icing (see Index).

# Decorated Fondant Candies

Among the recipes in this cookbook are treasured favorites from women to whom candy making is a hobby. One of these contributors, a home economist-homemaker, the wife of a north central Iowa farmer, teaches a course in candy making every autumn at her local YWCA. Her pupils admire her decorated fondant specials and especially her festive fondant mints.

She uses molds to shape many of these candies. Some of them are rubber, others are flexible plastic. They come in sets, which she sometimes cuts apart with kitchen scissors to divide with other candy makers. Among her favorite molds are those shaped like bells, which she uses for the Yuletide season, wedding receptions and bridal showers; diplomas, for high school graduation festivities; booties, for baby showers; hearts, for Valentine functions, and rose shapes—the flower candies are pretty for parties for any occasion.

This Iowa woman recently made and decorated 200 fondant candies for a big community gathering. She says she can keep them in fine condition up to two weeks; she recommends arranging the candies in single layers in shallow cardboard boxes, and keeping them covered.

The ingredients for fondant candies are inexpensive; it costs about 15 to 20 cents to make 50 candies. The greater expense is the time you spend in making and decorating them. You do divide the work, though, because you make the fondant ahead. You can go a step farther and shape and decorate the candies and put them in the freezer until needed. Let them thaw before uncovering.

When the shaped candies are set, you remove them from the molds and add decorative touches with Royal Icing. You can flavor and tint it with extracts and food colors, and put it through a decorating tube, using tiny tips.

Here is the fondant recipe this Iowa farm woman likes best, with directions for making her decorated candies. We include for good measure some of her most praised variations.

## DECORATED FONDANT CANDIES

*Festive candies brighten parties—no wonder they're hostess favorites*

| | |
|---|---|
| 2 c. sugar | Food color, as desired |
| 1 c. water | Glycerin |
| ⅛ tsp. cream of tartar | Royal Icing |
| ½ tsp. vanilla, or ¼ tsp. peppermint or wintergreen extract | |

Combine sugar, water and cream of tartar in 2-qt. heavy saucepan. Cook over medium heat, stirring constantly, until sugar is dissolved. When mixture comes to a boil, cover saucepan and let cook 3 minutes. Remove lid and cook candy mixture without stirring to the soft ball stage (236°). If sugar crystals form on sides of pan, wipe them off.

Remove from heat and pour onto platter cooled with cold water. Let stand without moving until center top of fondant does not stick when gently touched with finger and bottom of platter feels lukewarm. It takes about 25 minutes for it to cool. (If in a hurry, pour fondant into 2 water-cooled glass pie pans or platters instead of onto 1 platter. It will cool in about 15 minutes.)

Stir and work fondant with spatula until it becomes creamy and white. Knead smooth with hands. If you want to flavor parts of the fondant differently, divide in 3 parts. Add flavoring extract and food color to each as desired; then knead to distribute. (The amount of flavoring listed with ingredients is for the entire batch. If you divide the fondant, also divide the amount of flavoring you add to each part.)

Place each part in a small plastic bag, close tightly and store in the refrigerator at least 24 hours, or for several days. (Fondant keeps a long time at this stage, but if you want to store it several weeks instead of days, add the food color and flavoring when you are ready to shape the candies.)

When you are ready to shape the candies, place a plastic bag of fondant in top of double boiler and set it over the lower section containing water heated to 175°. (You don't have to stir fondant in a bag as it melts, nor worry about it crystallizing on sides of pan.)

Meanwhile, prepare molds by coating them with glycerin. They must be ready when the fondant is melted.

When fondant is melted, lift out plastic bag. Quickly snip a small opening in one corner. The bag will be hot to handle, so either drop bag of fondant into another plastic bag (also with corner clipped), or into a funnel made of waxed paper or plastic wrap, or into a pastry bag if you own one.

Squeeze melted fondant into molds. As soon as candy is cool and set, remove from molds. (If fondant gets too cool, return bag of it to double boiler over warm water to melt again.) If candies have rough or pointed bottoms, turn them over as soon as removed from molds to flatten bottoms and make a smooth surface.

Decorate cooled candies with Royal Icing put through decorating tube. For Christmas, mold bell-shaped candies from white fondant and decorate each with 2 green holly leaves of green-tinted Royal Icing (made with leaf tip) and tiny red icing dots for holly berries. Trim fondant patties with tinted or white icing flowers, or as you like for bridal showers and wedding receptions. Or decorate bell-shaped fondant with yellow (gold) ribbons, or with the bride's colors for wedding bells. Makes about 1 pound fondant.

**Royal Icing** Beat 1 egg white and ¼ tsp. cream of tartar, adding about ½ package (½ lb.) confectioners sugar, sifted, a little at a time or until peaks with a break form, but do not curl. Add a few drops of vanilla or other flavoring and tint as desired. Keep covered with damp cloth or tight lid until used.

## Variations

**Candies without Melting Fondant** Shape fondant with hands into small balls. Dust with cornstarch if necessary to prevent sticking. Also dust mold with cornstarch. Press fondant into mold and pop out. (You can manage with one mold because the fondant sets quickly.) Turn all hand-molded candies over to dry on other side.

**Snowballs** Shape fondant around little nut pieces to make small balls. Dip in slightly beaten egg white and then roll in flaked coconut. (Or make Nut Balls by substituting finely chopped nuts for coconut.)

**Forget-me-not Bonbons** Dip small ovals of fondant in melted fondant. When coating is set, make a simple flower of tinted icing on each piece with the decorating tube and a forget-me-not tip.

**Pastel Bonbons** Shape fondant in small ovals and dip in melted pink or green confection coating (see Index). A few of these candies add charm to your gift box.

## COCONUT KISSES

*No-cook potato candy goes glamorous when coated with chocolate*

| | |
|---|---|
| 1 lb. confectioners sugar | 3 tblsp. nonfat dry milk powder |
| 3 tblsp. instant mashed potato granules | 1 tblsp. butter |
| | 1½ tsp. almond extract |
| 6 tblsp. boiling water | 1 (4 oz.) can shredded coconut |
| ¼ tsp. salt | |

Sift confectioners sugar into 2-qt. bowl and set aside.

Prepare mashed potatoes according to package directions, using water, salt and dry milk powder. Add butter and almond extract.

Make a well in confectioners sugar; add warm potato mixture. Gradually work sugar in; mixture will liquefy at first, then thicken. Continue working in sugar and beating until mixture is thick enough to hold its shape, adding a little more sugar, 1 tblsp. at a time, if necessary.

Mix in coconut. Drop by spoonfuls onto waxed paper. Makes about 3 dozen pieces, or 1½ pounds.

N O T E : Candy may be made into balls in palm of hand, then rolled at once in toasted coconut. Or cool the candy balls until set, then cover with chocolate confection coating or dipping chocolate (see Index).

## SWEET POTATO CANDY

*You'll enjoy this tasty sweet from Mexican candy kitchens*

| | |
|---|---|
| 1 medium unpeeled sweet potato | 1½ c. finely cut or ground nuts |
| ¼ tsp. salt | ¾ c. finely cut or ground |
| 2 lbs. confectioners sugar | light raisins |
| 1 c. flaked coconut | 1 tsp. vanilla or rum extract |

Boil, bake or steam potato until tender; peel and put through food mill or sieve to remove any fibrous bits (you should have 1 c.). Turn into a 2-qt. bowl; add salt. Gradually add 1 lb. sugar; mixture will liquefy at first, then thicken.

After the first pound of sugar is worked in, add half of each: coconut, nuts and raisins. Add remaining coconut, nuts and raisins alternately with remaining 1 lb. sugar. Add vanilla. Mix until well blended.

Turn mixture out onto a marble slab, baking sheet or other surface and knead (this also can be done in a bowl if it's big enough).

Line two 12″ lengths of aluminum foil with waxed paper; dust lightly with additional confectioners sugar or coconut. Divide candy in half. With lightly buttered palms, pick up candy and form into a ball, then into a short roll in the hands. Place on waxed paper and continue to roll, working from center to both ends, holding paper firm with one hand while the other continues rolling until candy is about 1″ in diameter. Roll up firmly in waxed paper and foil and chill several hours.

Repeat rolling with other half of candy. To serve, cut in slices. Makes about 48 pieces, or 3 pounds.

## Variation

**Chocolate Easter Eggs**  Form Sweet Potato Candy in small egg shapes and dip in melted chocolate (see Chocolate for dipping in Index).

# Homemade Candy Bars—
## Quick, Easy and Delicious

Our brand new candy bars are for busy women who don't want to dip individual pieces of candy in chocolate, or who don't have time to do it. You'll be surprised how fast and easily you can turn out the appealing candy bars. You spread a coat of chocolate or butterscotch on waxed paper, cover it with one of our good fillings, and spread another coating on top. When firm you cut the candy into bars—the results are amazing and delicious.

These homemade candy bars travel successfully because they lie flat in a box. Their individual plastic wrap or aluminum foil wrappers keep the fillings fresh and protect the bars against jostling from rough handling in the mail. The bars do not break or crumble easily.

Since the idea of homemade candy bars is new, they'll attract attention and sell well at food bazaars.

They're a nice addition to the lunch box because they eat well out of hand. You can make almost a month's supply, 24 bars, at a time, if you cut them the size we suggest, about 2½ × 1". (You can, of course, cut the candy into smaller pieces, like fudge.)

We recommend that you do not make these candy bars in hot humid weather.

## CHOCOLATE COATING FOR CANDY BARS

*Smooth and glossy dress-up for candy*

1 (6 oz.) pkg. chocolate chips (1 c.)
2 tblsp. vegetable shortening

Melt chocolate chips and shortening over hot water. Stir until smooth. Use as directed in the following candy bar recipes. Makes enough to coat 24 (2½ × 1") candy bars (an 8" square of candy).

## Variations

**Milk Chocolate Coating** Substitute 1 (6 oz.) pkg. milk chocolate chips for the chocolate chips.

**Mint Chocolate Coating** Substitute 1 (6 oz.) pkg. mint-flavored chocolate chips for the chocolate chips.

**Butterscotch Coating** Substitute 1 (6 oz.) pkg. butterscotch-flavored morsels for the chocolate chips.

## BUTTERSCOTCH SCRAMBLE BARS

*Crisp, crunchy and ever so good*

1 (6 oz.) pkg. butterscotch-
flavored morsels (1 c.)
2 tblsp. shortening
½ c. confectioners sugar
1 c. salted Spanish peanuts

1 c. chow mein noodles,
slightly crushed
Chocolate Coating for Candy
Bars

Melt butterscotch pieces with shortening over hot water. Stir in confectioners sugar, then add the peanuts and chow mein noodles. Cool to lukewarm.

Spread half of Chocolate Coating for Candy Bars on waxed paper to make an 8″ square. (Place an 8″ square pan on the waxed paper and mark around it with a pencil to determine size.) Slide waxed paper with chocolate onto a baking sheet and place in refrigerator a few minutes, or until chocolate is firm. Remove from refrigerator.

Spoon filling several places over the coating. Then carefully spread it evenly to cover coating. With a metal spatula, smooth top and sides of filling.

Spread remaining half of coating over filling to cover.

Set aside until candy is firm and until it separates easily from waxed paper. (To hasten setting, place in refrigerator.)

Cut in 2½ ×1″ bars, or in any size desired. Wrap individually in plastic wrap or aluminum foil. Makes 24 bars.

## MACAROON FRUIT BARS

*Chocolate coating enhances bright color of filling and adds flavor*

1 (15 oz.) can sweetened
    condensed milk (1⅓ c.)
1 (3 oz.) pkg. strawberry
    flavor gelatin
1 (14 oz.) pkg. flaked coconut
    (4⅔ c.)

½ tsp. almond extract
Chocolate Coating for Candy
    Bars

Combine sweetened condensed milk (not evaporated) and gelatin. Stir in coconut and almond extract.

Spread half of Chocolate Coating for Candy Bars on waxed paper to make an 8″ square. (Place an 8″ square pan on waxed paper and mark around it with a pencil to determine size.) Slide waxed paper with chocolate onto a baking sheet and place in refrigerator a few minutes, or until chocolate is firm. Remove.

Spoon filling several places over the coating. Then carefully spread it evenly to cover coating. With a metal spatula, smooth top and sides of filling.

Spread remaining half of coating over filling to cover.

Set aside until candy is firm (candy bars made with this no-cook filling take longer to set than many other bars) and until it separates easily from waxed paper. (To hasten setting, place in refrigerator.)

Cut in 2½ ×1″ bars, or in any size desired. Wrap individually in plastic wrap or aluminum foil. Makes 24 bars.

NOTE: You can substitute cherry, raspberry, lime or other flavor gelatins for the strawberry, and cookie coconut for the flaked.

## PEANUT CREME BARS

*You can use salted mixed nuts instead of peanuts—chop large nuts*

¼ c. butter
⅓ c. dairy half-and-half
⅓ c. sugar
1 tsp. vanilla

3 c. confectioners sugar
1½ c. salted Spanish peanuts
Chocolate Coating for Candy
    Bars

Combine butter, dairy half-and-half and sugar in 1½-qt. heavy saucepan. Bring to a boil, stirring constantly. Boil 3 minutes.

Stir in vanilla, confectioners sugar and peanuts. Cool to luke-warm.

Spread half of Chocolate Coating for Candy Bars on waxed paper to make an 8" square. (Place an 8" square pan on waxed paper and mark around it with a pencil to determine size.) Slide waxed paper with chocolate onto a baking sheet and place in refrigerator a few minutes, or until chocolate is firm. Remove.

Spoon filling several places over the coating. Then carefully spread it evenly to cover coating. With a metal spatula, smooth top and sides of filling. (If filling is too thick to spread on chocolate coating, add enough half-and-half, about 1 tblsp., to make spreading consistency.)

Spread remaining half of coating over filling to cover.

Set aside until candy is firm and until it separates easily from waxed paper. (To hasten setting, place in refrigerator.)

Cut in 2½ ×1" bars, or in any size desired. Wrap individually in plastic wrap or aluminum foil. Makes 24 bars.

## ALMOND BARK BARS

*Wonderful flavors—creamy almond bark candy and chocolate*

1 lb. white confection coating (see Index)
¼ c. dairy half-and-half
½ c. sliced or chopped unblanched almonds
¼ tsp. almond extract
Chocolate Coating for Candy Bars

Combine confection coating and half-and-half; stir over hot water until coating melts. Stir in almonds and almond extract. Cool to lukewarm.

Spread half of Chocolate Coating for Candy Bars on waxed paper to make an 8" square. (Place an 8" square pan on the waxed paper and mark around it with a pencil to determine size.) Slide waxed paper with chocolate onto a baking sheet and place in refrigerator a few minutes, or until chocolate is firm. Remove.

Spoon filling several places over the coating. Then carefully spread it evenly to cover coating. With a metal spatula, smooth top and sides of filling.

Spread remaining half of coating over filling to cover.

Set aside until candy is firm and until it separates easily from waxed paper. (To hasten setting, place in refrigerator.)

Cut in 2½ ×1" bars, or in any size desired. Wrap individually in plastic wrap or aluminum foil. Makes 24 bars.

## DATE CRISPIE BARS

*Luscious crunchy filling attracts loyal supporters for these bars*

½ c. butter
½ c. sugar
1¼ c. halved dates (8 oz.)
1½ c. oven-toasted rice cereal

½ c. broken or chopped nuts
Chocolate Coating for Candy
Bars

Combine butter, sugar and dates in 2-qt. heavy saucepan. Cook over medium heat, stirring constantly, until mixture thickens. Remove from heat and stir in cereal and nuts. Cool to lukewarm.

Spread half of Chocolate Coating for Candy Bars on waxed paper to make an 8″ square. (Place an 8″ square pan on the waxed paper and mark around it with a pencil to determine size.) Slide waxed paper with chocolate onto a baking sheet and place in refrigerator a few minutes, or until chocolate is firm. Remove.

Spoon filling several places over the coating. Then carefully spread it evenly to cover coating. With a metal spatula, smooth top and sides of filling.

Spread remaining half of coating over filling to cover.

Set aside until candy is firm and until it separates easily from waxed paper. (To hasten setting, place in refrigerator.)

Cut in 2½×1″ bars, or in any size desired. Wrap individually in plastic wrap or aluminum foil. Makes 24 bars.

## DATE CONFECTION BARS

*The filling for these bars is thin but rich with a caramel-like taste*

¼ c. butter (½ stick)
1 c. brown sugar
1 egg
1 c. halved dates

¾ c. chopped nuts
Chocolate Coating for Candy
Bars

Combine butter, sugar, egg and dates in 1-qt. heavy saucepan. Bring to a boil over medium heat, stirring constantly. Boil 5 minutes. Cool almost completely, then stir in nuts.

Spread half of Chocolate Coating for Candy Bars on waxed paper to make an 8″ square. (Place an 8″ square pan on the waxed paper and mark around it with a pencil to determine size.) Slide waxed paper with chocolate onto a baking sheet and place in refrigerator a few minutes, or until chocolate is firm. Remove.

Spoon filling several places over the coating. Then carefully spread it evenly to cover coating. With a metal spatula, smooth top and sides of filling.

Spread remaining half of coating over filling to cover.

Set aside until candy is firm and until it separates easily from waxed paper. (To hasten setting, place in refrigerator.)

Cut in 2½×1" bars, or in any size desired. Wrap individually in plastic wrap or aluminum foil. Makes 24 bars.

## CARAMEL NUT BARS

*Top choice of several taste-testers*

1 (14 or 16 oz.) pkg. caramels
¼ c. butter (½ stick)
¼ c. dairy half-and-half
2 c. confectioners sugar

¾ c. chopped walnuts
Chocolate Coating for Candy
  Bars

Melt caramels (light or dark—some packages contain both kinds) and butter with dairy half-and-half in 2-qt. heavy saucepan over low heat. Stir occasionally. When completely melted, stir in confectioners sugar.

Remove from heat and add nuts. Cool to lukewarm before spreading.

Spread half of Chocolate Coating for Candy Bars on waxed paper to make an 8" square. (Place an 8" square pan on the waxed paper and mark around it with a pencil to determine size.) Slide waxed paper with chocolate onto a baking sheet and place in refrigerator a few minutes, or until chocolate is firm. Remove.

Spoon filling several places over the coating. Then carefully spread it evenly to cover coating. With a metal spatula, smooth top and sides of filling.

Spread remaining half of coating over filling to cover.

Set aside until candy is firm and until it separates easily from waxed paper. (To hasten setting, place in refrigerator.)

Cut in 2½×1" bars, or in any size desired. Wrap individually in plastic wrap or aluminum foil. Makes 24 bars.

## MACAROON CANDY BARS

*Whole or halved filberts make a fine substitute for almonds*

1 (15 oz.) can sweetened
  condensed milk (1⅓ c.)
1 envelope unflavored gelatin
1 (14 oz.) pkg. flaked or cookie
  coconut (4¾ c.)

½ c. sliced or chopped
  unblanched almonds
Chocolate Coating for Candy
Bars

Combine condensed milk (not evaporated) and gelatin in 2-qt. heavy saucepan. Heat just to a boil, stirring constantly, to dissolve gelatin. Remove from heat. Stir in coconut and almonds. Cool to lukewarm.

Spread half of Chocolate Coating for Candy Bars on waxed paper to make an 8" square. (Place an 8" square pan on the waxed paper and mark around it with a pencil to determine size.) Slide waxed paper with chocolate onto a baking sheet and place in refrigerator a few minutes, or until chocolate is firm. Remove.

Spoon filling several places over the coating. Then carefully spread it evenly to cover coating. With a metal spatula, smooth top and sides of filling.

Spread remaining half of coating over filling to cover.

Set aside until candy is firm and until it separates easily from waxed paper. (To hasten setting, place in refrigerator.)

Cut in 2½ × 1" bars, or in any size desired. Wrap individually in plastic wrap or aluminum foil. Makes 24 bars.

## GERMAN FRUIT CANDY BARS

*Good with either chocolate or butterscotch coating; take your choice*

1 envelope unflavored gelatin
¼ c. water
1 c. ground dried apricots
1½ c. ground raisins
½ c. light corn syrup
1 tsp. rum extract

1 c. chopped nuts or cookie
  coconut
2 tblsp. grated orange peel
  (optional)
Chocolate or Butterscotch
Coating for Candy Bars

Soften gelatin in water. Heat over water, stirring constantly, until gelatin is dissolved. Combine with remaining ingredients, except coating. Cool to lukewarm.

Spread half of coating on waxed paper to make an 8" square.

(Place an 8" square pan on the waxed paper and mark around it with a pencil to determine size.) Slide waxed paper with coating onto a baking sheet and place in refrigerator a few minutes, or until it is firm. Remove.

Spoon filling several places over the coating. Then carefully spread it evenly to cover coating. With a metal spatula, smooth top and sides of filling.

Spread remaining half of coating over filling to cover.

Set aside until candy is firm and until it separates easily from waxed paper. (To hasten setting, place in refrigerator.)

Cut in 2½ × 1" bars, or in any size desired. Wrap individually in plastic wrap or aluminum foil. Makes 24 bars.

## SWISS NOUGAT BARS

*These and Pistachio Nougat Bars are aristocrats of candy bars*

¼ c. dairy half-and-half
½ c. sugar
¼ c. butter or margarine
  (½ stick)
⅛ tsp. salt
2 c. confectioners sugar

1 c. (about) halved filberts
  (3½ oz. pkg.)
½ tsp. almond extract
Chocolate Coating for Candy
Bars

Combine dairy half-and-half, sugar, butter and salt in 2-qt. heavy saucepan. Bring to a boil, stirring constantly. Boil 3 minutes. Remove from heat; stir in confectioners sugar, filberts and almond extract. Cool to lukewarm.

Spread half of Chocolate Coating for Candy Bars on waxed paper to make an 8" square. (Place an 8" square pan on the waxed paper and mark around it with a pencil to determine size.) Slide waxed paper with chocolate onto a baking sheet and place in refrigerator a few minutes, or until chocolate is firm. Remove.

Spoon filling several places over the coating. Then carefully spread it evenly to cover coating. (If filling is too thick to spread, stir in a little half-and-half.) With a metal spatula, smooth top and sides of filling.

Spread remaining half of coating over filling to cover.

Set aside until candy is firm and until it separates easily from waxed paper. (To hasten setting, place in refrigerator.)

Cut in 2½ × 1" bars, or in any size desired. Wrap individually in plastic wrap or aluminum foil. Makes 24 bars.

## Variations

**Pistachio Nougat Bars** Use ⅓ c. pistachio nuts instead of filberts and add 2 drops green food color. Follow directions for Swiss Nougat Bars.

**Brazilian Nougat Bars** Add 2 tsp. instant coffee powder to mixture before cooking, and substitute pecans for the filberts.

## PRALINE CANDY BARS

*Filling is praline-rich and sweet*

| | |
|---|---|
| 1 c. brown sugar | ¾ c. pecan halves |
| ¼ c. butter (½ stick) | 1 tsp. vanilla |
| 3 tblsp. milk | Chocolate Coating for Candy |
| 2 c. confectioners sugar | Bars |

Combine brown sugar, butter and milk in 2-qt. heavy saucepan. Bring to a boil, stirring constantly, and boil 3 minutes. Remove from heat and stir in remaining ingredients, except coating. Cool to lukewarm.

Spread half of Chocolate Coating for Candy Bars on waxed paper to make an 8″ square. (Place an 8″ square pan on the waxed paper and mark around it with a pencil to determine size.) Slide waxed paper with chocolate onto a baking sheet and place in refrigerator a few minutes, or until chocolate is firm. Remove.

Spoon filling several places over the coating. Then carefully spread it evenly to cover coating. (Thin with a little milk if necessary for a creamy filling of spreading consistency.) With a metal spatula, smooth top and sides of filling.

Spread remaining half of coating over filling to cover.

Set aside until candy is firm and until it separates easily from waxed paper. (To hasten setting, place in refrigerator.)

Cut in 2½ × 1″ bars, or in any size desired. Wrap individually in plastic wrap or aluminum foil. Makes 24 bars.

## FRENCH CREME CANDY BARS

*Creamy, fondant-type filling has delicate coffee flavor undertones*

¼ c. butter (½ stick)
½ c. sugar
¼ c. dairy half-and-half
⅛ tsp. salt
½ tsp. instant coffee powder
¼ c. chocolate chips
1 c. miniature marshmallows

2 c. confectioners sugar
½ c. whole unblanched
   almonds (3¼ oz. pkg.)
½ tsp. almond extract
Chocolate Coating for Candy
   Bars

Combine butter, sugar, dairy half-and-half, salt and coffee powder in 2-qt. heavy saucepan. Bring to a boil, stirring occasionally; boil 3 minutes. Remove from heat and stir in chocolate chips and marshmallows. Then stir in confectioners sugar, almonds and almond extract. Cool until lukewarm.

Spread half of Chocolate Coating for Candy Bars on waxed paper to make an 8″ square. (Place an 8″ square pan on the waxed paper and mark around it with a pencil to determine size.) Slide waxed paper with chocolate onto a baking sheet and place in refrigerator a few minutes, or until chocolate is firm. Remove.

Spoon filling several places over the coating. Then carefully spread it evenly to cover coating. (Thin filling if necessary with additional half-and-half until creamy and of spreading consistency.) With a metal spatula, smooth top and sides of filling.

Spread remaining half of coating over filling to cover.

Set aside until candy is firm and until it separates easily from waxed paper. (To hasten setting, place in refrigerator.)

Cut in 2½ ×1″ bars, or in any size desired. Wrap individually in plastic wrap or aluminum foil. Makes 24 bars.

## SOUTHERN CANDY BARS

*Bars are rather thin but rich and full of country flavor*

2 eggs
⅔ c. sugar
⅓ c. butter
1 c. white raisins

1 c. cookie coconut
1 tsp. vanilla
Chocolate Coating for Candy
   Bars

Beat eggs and sugar until mixture thickens. Combine in 2-qt. heavy saucepan with butter and raisins. Cook over medium heat, stirring constantly, until mixture comes to a boil. Cook 2 to 3 minutes longer, or until mixture thickens. Remove from heat and stir in coconut and vanilla. Cool to lukewarm.

Spread half of Chocolate Coating for Candy Bars on waxed paper to make an 8″ square. (Place an 8″ square pan on the waxed paper and mark around it with a pencil to determine size.) Slide waxed paper with chocolate onto a baking sheet and place in refrigerator a few minutes, or until chocolate is firm. Remove.

Spoon filling several places over the coating. Then carefully spread it evenly to cover coating. With a metal spatula, smooth top and sides of filling.

Spread remaining half of coating over filling to cover.

Set aside until candy is firm and until it separates easily from waxed paper. (To hasten setting, place in refrigerator.)

Cut in 2½ × 1″ bars, or in any size desired. Wrap individually in plastic wrap or aluminum foil. Makes 24 bars.

## MALLOW CANDY BARS

*Double marshmallow/chocolate treat*

| | |
|---|---|
| 32 regular marshmallows | 2 tblsp. butter |
| ½ c. milk chocolate pieces | 2 c. miniature marshmallows |
| (half of a 6 oz. pkg.) | Mint or Milk Chocolate |
| ¼ c. milk | Coating for Candy Bars |

Melt regular marshmallows with milk chocolate pieces and milk in top of double boiler over hot water, stirring frequently. When melted, stir in butter. Remove from heat and cool almost completely. Stir in miniature marshmallows.

Spread half of coating on waxed paper to make an 8″ square. (Place an 8″ square pan on the waxed paper and mark around it with a pencil to determine size.) Slide waxed paper with chocolate onto a baking sheet and place in refrigerator a few minutes, or until it is firm. Remove.

Spoon filling several places over the coating. Then carefully spread it evenly to cover coating. With a metal spatula, smooth top and sides of filling.

Spread remaining half of coating over filling to cover.

Set aside until candy is firm and until it separates easily from waxed paper. (To hasten setting, place in refrigerator.)

Cut in 2½ × 1″ bars, or in any size desired. Wrap individually in plastic wrap or aluminum foil. Makes 24 bars.

## PEANUT CRUNCH BARS

*A favorite with boys of all ages*

1 c. light corn syrup
½ c. sugar
1 (6 oz.) pkg. butterscotch-
flavored morsels (1 c.)
1 c. oven-toasted rice cereal

1 c. peanut butter
½ c. salted peanuts (optional)
Chocolate Coating for Candy
Bars

Bring corn syrup and sugar to a full boil in 2-qt. heavy saucepan, stirring constantly. Boil 3 minutes. Remove from heat and stir in butterscotch pieces; then add rice cereal, peanut butter and peanuts. Cool almost completely before spreading.

Spread half of Chocolate Coating for Candy Bars on waxed paper to make an 8″ square. (Place an 8″ square pan on the waxed paper and mark around it with a pencil to determine size.) Slide waxed paper with chocolate onto a baking sheet and place in refrigerator a few minutes, or until chocolate is firm. Remove.

Spoon filling several places over the coating. Then carefully spread it evenly to cover coating. With a metal spatula, smooth top and sides of filling.

Spread remaining half of coating over filling to cover. Refrigerate until set.

Cut in 2½ × 1″ bars, or in any size desired. Wrap individually in plastic wrap or aluminum foil. Makes 24 bars.

## Variations

You can layer one filling on top of another to make double-thick candy bars. Here are some combinations our taste panel liked:

Caramel Nut and Swiss Nougat (without nuts)
Caramel (without nuts) and Peanut Creme
Date Confection and Swiss Nougat (without nuts)
Caramel (without nuts) and filling for Mallow Candy Bars
Caramel (without nuts) and French Creme

# Crisp Nut Brittles

Brittles are correctly named—they're very crisp. Peanut brittle is the most famous one but other nuts and coconut also are good in the candy. While they're easy to make, there are a few rules that it pays to heed:

Remove sugar crystals from the sides of the saucepan if they appear during the cooking (see Index for directions in "How to Make Perfect Candy at Home").

Mix the nuts into the hot candy quickly and stir no more than necessary to distribute them. This helps to avoid sugary candy. It's also a good idea to warm the nuts first so they will not cool the candy so much that you will be unable to pour it in a thin sheet. One way is to put the nuts in a slow (250°) oven while the candy cooks. They'll also taste better if toasted.

Cut or break the nuts instead of chopping them on a board. The fine dust that forms in the chopping makes brittles cloudy.

Pour the cooked candy onto a lightly buttered slab or baking sheet. Do not scrape the pan. Spread brittle out with a spatula. As soon as it is cool enough to touch, lift the edges and pull to stretch the brittle thin.

If the brittle is sugary, you can redeem it. Put it in a saucepan with ¾ c. hot water and 2 tblsp. light corn syrup. Heat slowly until candy dissolves. Then cook it again to the temperature specified in the recipe. Pour and stretch it as described.

Store brittles in airtight containers or tightly closed plastic bags in the freezer or a cold place. They often become sticky if exposed to the air, especially when it's warm and humid.

## American Peanut Brittle

Peanut brittle is as American as the Stars and Stripes. Country women make it in different ways. We give you three of their favorites, using raw, salted and roasted peanuts. Choose the one that appeals to you the most. All make wonderful candy.

With Classic Peanut Brittle you caramelize the sugar for a superlative, true caramel flavor. The other two recipes include light corn syrup as an ingredient, which helps to prevent candy from becoming sugary. You can use either the larger Virginia or the smaller Spanish peanuts, but if you choose the larger kind, remove the red skins.

While some candy makers try to cut peanut brittle, it's often impossible to do it. The classic way is to break it into irregular pieces.

**To Blanch Peanuts** Cover peanuts with boiling water and let stand 3 minutes. Drain, run cold water over them and remove the skins. Dry thoroughly before using.

## CLASSIC PEANUT BRITTLE

*Old-fashioned way to make up-to-date brittle super delicious*

| | |
|---|---|
| 1 tblsp. butter or margarine | ¼ tsp. salt |
| 1¼ c. salted peanuts, broken or cut in pieces | 2⅓ c. sugar |

Melt butter in small saucepan over very low heat. Add peanuts and salt. Let warm.

Put sugar in 12″ heavy skillet over medium heat. Stir constantly until sugar melts into a light golden brown syrup (use care not to scorch). Quickly stir warmed peanut mixture into syrup.

Pour onto lightly buttered large surface at once (a large baking sheet makes a satisfactory surface, as does an inverted large pan). Spread out with spatula.

With a big spoon and fingers, pull candy into a thin sheet.

Cool; then break in pieces with a knife handle. Makes 1¼ pounds.

## VIRGINIA PEANUT BRITTLE

*You make this paper-thin, light-colored brittle with raw nuts—a favorite of peanut growers' wives*

| | |
|---|---|
| 2 c. sugar | ¼ tsp. salt |
| 1 c. light corn syrup | 1 tsp. butter or margarine |
| 1 c. water | ¼ tsp. baking soda |
| 2 c. unroasted peanuts, cut in pieces | |

Combine sugar, corn syrup and water in a 12″ heavy skillet.

Cook slowly over medium heat, stirring constantly until sugar is dissolved. Continue cooking until mixture reaches the soft ball stage (236°).

Add peanuts and salt; cook to just beyond the soft crack stage (290 to 300°). Add butter and soda, stirring to blend (mixture will foam).

Pour onto 2 large buttered baking sheets or 2 inverted buttered large pans. Lift candy around edges with spatula and run spatula under candy to cool it partially and keep it from sticking. While candy is still warm, but firm, turn it over and pull edges to make the brittle thinner in the center. When cold, break into pieces with knife handle. Makes about 2¼ pounds.

## SALTED PEANUT BRITTLE DE LUXE

*You need a candy thermometer for this recipe from an Iowa farm woman*

| | |
|---|---|
| 2 c. sugar | 3 tblsp. butter or margarine |
| 1 c. light corn syrup | 1 tsp. vanilla |
| ¼ c. water | 2 tsp. baking soda |
| 1½ c. salted peanuts | |

Combine sugar, corn syrup and water in a 3-qt. heavy saucepan; mix well. Cook over medium heat, stirring constantly, until sugar dissolves. Continue cooking, stirring frequently to prevent scorching, until mixture reaches 285°. Remove from heat at once.

Stir in peanuts and butter, and cook, stirring constantly with thermometer, until mixture reaches 295°. Remove from heat at once.

Add vanilla and baking soda, stir to blend (work fast). Mixture will foam.

Pour onto well-buttered marble slab or 2 large buttered baking sheets. Spread out as thin as possible with spatula. As soon as brittle is cool enough so that you can work with it (about 5 minutes), turn it over and pull to stretch as thin as possible. When cold, break in pieces. Makes about 2 pounds.

## ALMOND BRITTLE

*A West Coast favorite—the sesame seed version comes from sweet shops in San Francisco's Chinatown, but you can make it at home*

⅓ c. butter                    1 c. whole blanched almonds
1 c. sugar                     ⅛ tsp. salt

Combine all ingredients in an 8″ heavy skillet. Cook over medium-high heat until sugar dissolves, stirring occasionally until almonds begin to pop and turn a light amber color. Remove from heat; pour onto chilled buttered baking sheet. Lift along one edge as brittle starts to cool and turn it over, stretching it as you turn (use a slightly greased asbestos mitt, if necessary).

When cold, break in pieces. Makes about 14 ounces.

N O T E : This brittle can be put through a food chopper, using coarse knife, and used as a topping for ice cream.

## *Variation*

**Sesame Seed Brittle**  Omit almonds; cook butter, sugar and salt in 2-qt. heavy saucepan. As syrup nears the hard crack stage (290 to 300°), add 1 c. sesame seeds. When they turn light amber in color, remove from heat, and pour at once into a buttered and chilled 9″ square pan. When cold, break in pieces.

## ALMOND BUTTER CRUNCH

*Make some Christmas Stars with this candy and almonds*

1½ c. blanched almond halves      1 tblsp. light corn syrup
¾ c. butter (1½ sticks)           3 tblsp. water
1½ c. sugar

To halve almonds, pour boiling water over nuts and simmer 2 minutes. Drain and split in halves.

Toast almonds on baking sheet in slow oven (300°) until golden brown.

Melt butter in 2-qt. heavy saucepan; add sugar, corn syrup and water. Cook to soft crack stage (290°) without stirring.

Remove from heat and pour in thin stream over nuts on baking sheet. Cool. Break into pieces. Makes about 1½ pounds.

*Variation*

**Christmas Stars** Arrange clusters of 5 toasted almond halves in star patterns on baking sheets. Drop teaspoonfuls of hot candy on clusters of almonds. Cool.

# Unsurpassable Filbert Brittle

Filberts grow in Oregon and candy makers there believe that confections featuring them can't be surpassed. They have a right to be proud of this brittle. If you can't find filberts in your markets, you can use either raw Spanish peanuts or salted peanuts as a substitute in the recipe for Filbert Brittle.

As with all brittle recipes, the trick is to prevent scorching and the formation of sugar crystals during the cooking. This recipe shows the way a home economics teacher controls these problems. All her friends recognize her as an expert candy maker.

She likes to pour the cooked brittle onto a warm marble slab, brushed with mineral oil, but you can use heavy duty foil, well oiled or buttered. To warm the marble, she lays her electric pad on it and turns on the electricity—an original idea.

### FILBERT BRITTLE

*A holiday treat in the Northwest—it's worth adoption across country*

| | |
|---|---|
| 4 c. whole or halved filberts | 2 tblsp. butter |
| 3 c. sugar | ½ tsp. salt |
| 1¼ c. light corn syrup | 1 tsp. baking soda |
| 1 c. boiling water | 1 tsp. vanilla |

Remove any excess or loose fibers from filberts, but do not remove skins.

Combine sugar, corn syrup and boiling water in 3-qt. heavy saucepan. Stir until sugar is dissolved, then cover and place over medium heat until syrup boils. Remove lid; insert candy thermometer and cook at medium boil to the soft ball stage (240°).

Add filberts all at once. Do not stir until mixture again boils (it might start a crystal). Then stir with a wooden spoon to keep nuts from scorching, using care not to touch sides of pan above surface of syrup, for the friction of spoon may cause crystals to fall into syrup and cause a coarse-grain candy.

Cook to the hard crack stage (310°), or even beyond it to 320°, at which stage sugar caramelizes and turns a dark golden color. Add butter; remove from heat at once. Then add salt, soda and vanilla, stirring in well.

Pour onto warm marble slab, brushed with mineral oil or butter, or onto buttered heavy duty foil. Pour brittle so it spreads out as thinly as possible. Work a buttered or oiled spatula under one side of brittle and turn it over. Pull the brittle as thin as possible. (A heatproof mitt is helpful in turning and pulling brittle.)

Let cool; then break in pieces of eating size. Store in airtight containers. Place in freezer, refrigerator or other cold place. Makes 3 pounds.

## Variations

**Northwest Peanut Brittle**  Substitute 2¾ c. (1 lb.) raw Spanish peanuts for the filberts in Filbert Brittle.

**Salted Peanut Brittle**  Instead of the filberts, use 2 c. large red-skinned salted peanuts. Rub a handful at a time between paper towels and then sift to remove some of the salt. Omit the ½ tsp. salt, and proceed as directed in recipe for Filbert Brittle.

## SLOVAKIAN NUT CANDY

*This heirloom recipe calls for only two ingredients—nuts and sugar*

    1 c. ground nuts
    1 c. sugar

Put nuts through food chopper and measure before starting to melt sugar.

Place sugar in a 10″ heavy skillet and stir over medium heat until it melts and turns a light golden brown. Remove from heat at once.

Stir in nuts and pour onto buttered board. Roll with buttered rolling pin until very thin (17½ × 6″).

Cut at once in strips 2″ wide. Loosen strips from board with buttered spatula and cut with sharp knife on the diagonal to make diamonds. Makes ½ pound.

N O T E : Although the original recipe doesn't call for it, you may
want to add a pinch of salt.

## BRITTLE CHIP CANDY

*You put brittle through a food chopper, then coat with chocolate*

| | |
|---|---|
| 1 c. sugar | 1 (12 oz.) pkg. sweet milk |
| 1 c. unblanched almonds | chocolate, light or dark |

Combine sugar and nuts in a 10" heavy skillet (cast iron is good);
cook over low to medium heat, stirring occasionally until sugar
melts and nuts begin to make popping sounds. Remove from heat;
pour at once onto a buttered dinner plate or pan. Spread candy
out, separating nuts as much as possible (nuts will be in a thin
brittle). Cool.

When completely cool, put through food chopper, using medium
knife.

Meanwhile, melt chocolate in top of double boiler over hot water,
stirring occasionally to prevent chocolate settling to bottom. When
melted, add ground candy all at once; stir to combine.

Pour at once into a shallow 11×7" pan lined on bottom with
waxed paper (candy should be about ¼" thick). When cool, cut
in 1" squares with sharp knife. Makes 6 to 7 dozen pieces, or 1
pound.

## Variation

**Filbert Brittle Chip Candy** Instead of the almonds in Brittle Chip
Candy, substitute unblanched filberts. Be sure to remove any
loose pieces of husk. Filberts may be cut in halves, if desired.

## CEREAL/RAISIN BRITTLE

*An ideal sweet for children*

| | |
|---|---|
| 3 c. seedless light or dark raisins | 1 c. sugar |
| 1¼ c. puffed rice cereal | 1 tblsp. molasses |
| 1¼ c. high protein cereal | 2 tblsp. butter |
| ½ c. water | ½ tsp. salt |
| ½ c. light corn syrup | ¼ tsp. baking soda |

Remove any stems or hard pieces from raisins; place in greased
13×9×2" pan.

Measure cereals into a 4-qt. bowl; place in very slow oven (250°) to crisp and keep warm. Also place raisins in oven to warm.

Combine water, corn syrup and sugar in 2-qt. heavy saucepan. Stir to mix, then bring to a boil over medium heat. If sugar crystals form on sides of pan, wipe them off. Cook almost to the hard crack stage (290 to 300°). Add molasses, butter and salt and remove from heat. Add soda; stir vigorously to combine all ingredients and to stir down foaming action.

Combine raisins and cereals in bowl; quickly pour hot syrup over, mixing thoroughly. Turn out at once into the warmed and buttered raisin pan; with back of buttered spatula, flatten evenly to about ⅜" thickness. While cooling, cut in 1" squares. Makes about 9 dozen pieces, or 2¼ pounds.

# Butterscotch and Toffee

Butterscotch is really a brittle—but with one difference. It always contains a goodly amount of butter. That's the secret of why it tastes so marvelous.

Toffee is in this great candy family, too. It's less brittle and somewhat thicker than its relatives—and plenty good. Pour it out as directed, to cool until firm—then break it into irregular pieces. Or, if you prefer neat squares or rectangles of toffee, mark the warm candy deeply with a knife. Then, when it is cool, you can break it along the marked lines in evenly shaped pieces. Some candy makers pour hot toffee onto lightly buttered baking sheets instead of into pans. However, if you want to mark the candy into evenly shaped pieces, you'll find that the sides of the pan help keep the edges straight.

## OLD-FASHIONED BUTTERSCOTCH

*Butter-smooth with a crunch*

| | |
|---|---|
| 2 c. sugar | 2 tblsp. water |
| ¼ c. light corn syrup | 2 tblsp. vinegar |
| ½ c. butter (1 stick) | |

Combine all ingredients in 2-qt. heavy saucepan. Stir and cook over medium heat until sugar is dissolved, then reduce heat and cook at a medium boil, stirring as needed to control foaming and to avoid sticking as mixture thickens. If sugar crystals form on sides of pan, wipe them off. Cook to the hard crack stage (300°).

Remove from heat and let stand 1 minute.

Meanwhile, butter 2 sheets of aluminum foil and place on 2 baking sheets. Quickly drop teaspoonfuls of butterscotch onto foil, making patties about 1" in diameter. Space them ½" apart. If candy thickens so that it will not drop easily, set pan in hot water until it again is workable. Makes about 6 dozen patties or 1¼ pounds.

## Variations

**Brown Sugar Butterscotch**   Substitute 2 c. brown sugar, firmly packed, for the white sugar and ¼ c. molasses for the corn syrup in Old-Fashioned Butterscotch. Cook and handle as directed in recipe.

NOTE: Instead of dropping butterscotch onto buttered foil, pour it into a well-buttered 8″ square pan. When partly cool, mark in squares with a knife; turn out onto buttered foil while still warm and slightly pliable. (A knife or spatula inserted along one side will help release it.) When butterscotch has hardened, tap it with a mallet or wooden spoon to break candy into pieces along the lines.

**Perfect Butterscotch Patties**   Instead of dropping butterscotch onto oiled or buttered foil or pan, spoon it into lightly oiled or buttered tiny muffin-pan cups (1¼″ in diameter). Make thin patties. Remove when cold. This tip comes from a creative Iowa farmer's wife, who makes wonderful candies and takes pictures of some of the beauties before her family and friends enjoy eating them. She adds a little yellow food color to give the patties a more interesting appearance.


## BUTTER CRUNCH TOFFEE

*Flavor and crunchy texture make this candy a winner every time*

| | |
|---|---|
| 1 c. butter or margarine | ¾ c. broken nuts |
| (2 sticks) | 4 squares semisweet chocolate, |
| 1 c. sugar | melted |
| 2 tblsp. water | ¼ c. finely chopped nuts |
| 1 tblsp. light corn syrup | |

In 2-qt. heavy saucepan melt butter over low heat. Remove from heat and add sugar; stir until well blended. Return to low heat and stir rapidly until mixture reaches a full rolling boil. Add water and corn syrup; mix well.

Stir and cook over low heat to the soft crack stage (290°). Remove from heat and add ¾ c. nuts at once. Pour into lightly buttered 13×9×2″ pan and quickly spread with spatula.

When cool, remove from pan and place on waxed paper; spread

top with melted chocolate. Sprinkle with the finely chopped nuts. When chocolate is set, break in serving-size pieces. Makes 1¼ pounds.

## RAISIN/NUT TOFFEE

*Raisins are the happy surprise in this candy from California*

| | |
|---|---|
| 1 c. sugar | 1 c. seedless raisins |
| ½ c. water | 8 squares semisweet chocolate |
| ¾ c. butter (1½ sticks) | (8 oz. pkg.) |
| 1 tsp. vanilla | 1 c. finely chopped walnuts |

Combine sugar and water in 2-qt. heavy saucepan; cook over medium heat, stirring until syrup comes to a boil and sugar is dissolved. Slowly add butter and cook to the hard crack stage (300°). Remove from heat; add vanilla and raisins.

Pour into a buttered 13×9×2″ pan. When cold, remove from pan and place on waxed paper.

Meanwhile, melt chocolate over low heat, stirring constantly. Spread half of it on one side of candy; sprinkle with half of the nuts. Chill. Then turn toffee over and spread other side with remaining chocolate and sprinkle with remaining nuts. Cut or break in pieces. This candy improves on standing in airtight container with waxed paper between layers. Store in refrigerator. Makes about 1¾ pounds.

## DOUBLE ALMOND CRUNCH

*Toffee is chocolate-nut coated on both sides—it also contains nuts*

| | |
|---|---|
| 1 c. coarsely chopped almonds | 1 tblsp. light corn syrup |
| 1 c. finely chopped almonds | 3 tblsp. water |
| 1 c. butter (2 sticks) | 3 (4½ oz.) bars milk chocolate, |
| 1⅓ c. sugar | melted |

Spread almonds in separate shallow pans. Place in slow oven

*SPRING GIFT ASSORTMENT—Unusual sweets in luscious pastel colors fill a gift box that's perfect for a Mother's Day or Easter remembrance. Try coconut-coated Homemade Marshmallows, page 136, creamy Open House Mints, page 171, and Decorated Sugar Cubes, page 174.*

(300°) until nuts are delicately browned or until time to add them to candy. Watch carefully.

Meanwhile, melt butter over low heat in 2-qt. heavy saucepan; add sugar, corn syrup and water. Cook, stirring occasionally, to the hard crack stage (300°). Watch carefully after candy reaches 280°.

Quickly stir in warmed, toasted coarsely chopped almonds. Spread in ungreased 13×9×2″ pan. Cool thoroughly.

Turn onto waxed paper; spread top with half of chocolate and sprinkle with half of finely chopped almonds. Cover with waxed paper and turn over. Spread candy with remaining chocolate and sprinkle with remaining almonds. Set in cold place until chocolate is firm. Break in pieces. Makes 2½ pounds.

## ALMOND TOFFEE

*Try this almond candy—it's superb*

| | |
|---|---|
| 1 c. butter (½ lb. or 2 sticks) | 1¼ c. sugar |
| ¾ to 1 c. coarsely chopped blanched almonds | 1 (6 oz.) pkg. chocolate chips |

Melt butter over low heat in 3-qt. heavy saucepan, then add nuts and sugar. Turn heat to high and stir rapidly until color changes to a light caramel, about 5 minutes. Almonds will start to pop at this stage and mixture will have a compact appearance, yet be fluid enough to pour out. Do not overcook!

Remove from heat and pour at once into a slightly warm ungreased 13×9×2″ pan. Spread out as thinly and evenly as possible, to about a ⅜″ thickness (candy may not fill pan completely).

Distribute chocolate chips over hot candy and spread evenly when they have melted.

When cool, turn pan upside down on waxed paper; tap to release toffee. Break in bite-size pieces with a small household hammer. Or, turn candy chocolate side up and mark in squares or rectangles (with a French chef's knife, if available). Tap back of knife with hammer to cut in pieces. Makes about 96 pieces, or 1¾ pounds.

N O T E : About ¼ c. of the chopped almonds may be reserved and sprinkled over the melted chocolate. These should be chopped finer than those used in the toffee.

# Tempting Bark Candy

Most shoppers who linger over candy counters tend to stop at the trays of bark candy—they're almost irresistible. Barks are sheet candy that contains nuts. They are nut brittle. You might call them candied nuts—with more candy than nuts. They're simple to make in home kitchens.

The easiest method is to use confection coating—white, chocolate, pink or green—for the candy portion. As for nuts, you can use almonds, pecans, peanuts, filberts or cashews, or mixtures of them. All these nuts are best when toasted (directions follow). Walnuts also are good in barks and you need not toast them. If you chop the nuts or break them in pieces, you'll find it easier to spread the candy thin.

Use 2 c. melted confection coating to 1 c. nuts (unsalted). To melt the coating, cut it in small pieces and place in double boiler over boiling water; stir constantly until it is melted. Be sure to determine when the melted coating is cool enough (105°) to stir in the nuts. Use ½ tsp. vanilla with all nuts except almonds—with those use ¼ tsp. almond extract.

Spread the candy about ½″ thick on waxed paper. When it is cool, break it in pieces. If you want to keep the bark a few days, put it in tightly closed plastic bags or in an airtight container. Store in a cool place.

We give you a special "from-scratch" recipe for luscious Toasted Almond Bark followed by directions for making three treats using the confection coating. And here's how you toast the nuts:

**To Toast Nuts** Spread nuts in large shallow pan and heat in a slow oven (300°) until a light brown, about 10 minutes. Watch carefully. Then cool to room temperature before using.

## TOASTED ALMOND BARK

*Creamy candy with toasted almonds is easy to make and extra-good*

2 c. sugar
⅔ c. milk
1 tblsp. light corn syrup
¼ tsp. salt

2 tblsp. butter
1 tsp. vanilla
1 c. toasted unblanched almonds

Combine sugar, milk, corn syrup and salt in 2-qt. heavy saucepan. Cook, stirring constantly until sugar dissolves and mixture comes to a boil. Then cook without stirring to soft ball stage (234°).

Remove from heat; add butter, but do not stir. Let cool until lukewarm (110°). Then add vanilla. Beat until mixture thickens and is creamy. Add toasted almonds. Then spread about ½″ thick on waxed paper-lined baking sheet. Cool; break in pieces. Makes about 1½ pounds.

## DIPPED PRETZELS

*White-coated pretzels are crunchy and tasty—and toasted almonds in bark candy are a bonus sure to please everyone*

1 lb. white confection coating (see Index)
24 small pretzels

Cut coating in small pieces; place in double boiler over boiling water. Stir constantly until it is melted.

Cool until coating is 105° on candy thermometer. Set it over warm water of the same temperature.

Dip pretzels, one at a time, into melted coating to cover them. Place on waxed paper to dry. Use remaining coating to make Almond Bark.

N O T E : Unsalted pretzels will keep longer than the salted kind, but salted ones may be used.

**Almond Bark**  Add ¼ tsp. almond extract to remaining melted coating. Stir to mix, and stir in ½ c. unblanched almonds. Pour onto waxed paper. Let cool, then break in pieces. Makes 3 to 4 dozen pieces.

## NUT FLUFF LOG

*Roll candy, marshmallows and peanuts together for a treat*

½ lb. white confection coating          1 c. salted peanuts
  (see Index)                          1 c. miniature marshmallows
2 tblsp. milk

Combine coating and milk in top of double boiler; melt over boiling water. Stir until smooth. Remove from lower part of double boiler and stir in peanuts and marshmallows.

Divide mixture in half on two sheets of waxed paper. Shape each half in a 10″ log, using waxed paper to help in the shaping. Chill 30 minutes, or until set. To serve, cut in ½″ slices. Makes 2 logs, or about 40 pieces.

# Pralines

People away from home, homesick for friends and relatives left behind, also long for familiar foods unavailable in their new surroundings. Out of this yearning for pralines, or almonds coated with a sugar glaze, early French settlers in New Orleans created a new kind of pralines with the ingredients to be found in what now is Louisiana.

Instead of almonds, they used the native pecans (then called Western or Illinois nuts) and brown sugar. They christened the new candy pralines, in remembrance of the confection in France.

The candy caught on and to this day it's rare for a tourist in fascinating New Orleans to pass up pralines during his visit to the Crescent City. And in thousands of home kitchens across the country, women make pralines of one kind or another. Here are some of the favorite pralines of FARM JOURNAL readers:

## PRALINE PRIZE WINNERS

*This candy won blue ribbons for a Michigan woman. It's really good*

| | |
|---|---|
| 1 lb. light brown sugar | 1½ c. pecan halves |
| ⅛ tsp. salt | 1 tsp. vanilla |
| ¾ c. evaporated milk | |

Mix together all ingredients, except vanilla, in a 3-qt. heavy saucepan. Cook over medium heat, stirring constantly until sugar dissolves. Continue cooking to the soft ball stage (236°), stirring occasionally or constantly, as needed, to prevent sticking.

Remove from heat and let cool 5 minutes. Add vanilla.

Beat with a wooden spoon until candy begins to thicken. Drop rapidly from tablespoon onto waxed paper or aluminum foil. (If candy becomes too stiff to drop, stir in ½ tsp. hot water.) Makes 22 (2″) patties, or 1½ pounds.

## TWO-STEP PRALINES

*For a holiday look, drop into colored waxed paper candy cups*

*Step 1* (*Fondant*):

2 c. sugar                          2 tblsp. light corn syrup
1½ c. boiling water

Butter sides of a 2-qt. heavy saucepan. Combine all ingredients in it and cook over medium heat, stirring constantly until mixture comes to a boil.

Continue cooking without stirring to the soft ball stage (238°). Pour quickly onto a platter without scraping pan.

Cool without stirring or moving for 30 minutes. Mixture should feel lukewarm to the hand. Then work it with a wooden spoon until creamy and stiff; knead until free of lumps. Wrap well in foil or plastic wrap and refrigerate (you can keep it for several days). Makes about 1 cup, or enough for 2 batches of pralines.

*Step 2* (*Pralines*):

1½ c. light brown sugar             ½ c. Step 1 mixture
1 tblsp. light corn syrup           1 c. pecan halves
1 c. light cream or dairy half-     ½ tsp. salt
  and-half                          ½ tsp. vanilla
Few grains baking soda

Combine brown sugar, corn syrup, cream and soda in 2-qt. heavy saucepan. Cook, stirring constantly until mixture comes to a boil. Continue cooking, stirring only when necessary to prevent candy sticking to pan, to the soft ball stage (234°).

Remove from heat and immediately add the remaining ingredients. Stir gently until Step 1 mixture is completely blended in.

Drop from teaspoon onto waxed paper. If candy gets too stiff to drop, stir in a few drops of warm water. Store in airtight containers. Makes 27 pralines, or 1¼ pounds.

## TEXAS PRALINES

*Some pralines are sugary but these are creamy and big, Texas style*

3 c. light brown sugar              1 tsp. vanilla
1 c. dairy half-and-half            1 c. broken pecans, or about
3 tblsp. light or dark corn syrup     36 halves
⅓ c. butter

Combine sugar, half-and-half, corn syrup and butter in 3-qt.

heavy saucepan. Stir to combine; bring to a boil over medium-high heat; then reduce heat to medium-low, stirring occasionally to prevent scorching. Cook to the soft ball stage (238°). Remove from heat and cool to lukewarm (110°) without stirring.

Add vanilla; beat until mixture changes color and begins to thicken.

Quickly pour or dip with large spoon onto 2 waxed paper-lined baking sheets, making circles about 3½" in diameter; allow 6 to a baking sheet. If mixture sets too fast, add 1 tsp. or more hot water until patties again will spread when poured. Sprinkle 1 tsp. nuts or about 3 pecan halves over each. Makes 12 pralines, or about 1¾ pounds.

NOTE: You can pour praline mixture into a buttered 9" square pan. Sprinkle broken nuts on top (pecans or black walnuts) and press into the surface with a broad spatula. When cool, cut into 36 pieces.

## CREOLE CANDY

*This candy, made with confectioners sugar, is a relative of pralines*

| | |
|---|---|
| 2 c. sifted confectioners sugar | 1 c. pecan halves |
| ¼ c. butter (½ stick) | ¼ c. boiling water |
| ⅛ tsp. salt | ½ tsp. vanilla |

Combine all ingredients, except vanilla, in 2-qt. heavy saucepan. Bring to a boil. Continue cooking, stirring only to prevent scorching, to the soft ball stage (238°), about 5 minutes. Remove from heat.

Add vanilla; stir until mixture begins to thicken. Drop by teaspoonfuls onto waxed paper or into paper candy cups. Makes 20 pieces, or about 1 pound.

# Jellied Candies

The versatile performer in several unusual candies and confections is gelatin. There are two delights which we especially recommend: delicate Homemade Marshmallows, which mothers like to fix for their children; and the sparkling sweet that our taste-testers called "darling Candy Strawberries"—as fresh-tasting as they look. You can go fancy for a special party and buy marzipan strawberry leaves on (artificial) stems to stick in top of the candy berries, but we give you another choice for topknots for your "berries" too: almonds, tinted green. Tasty and pretty.

Among the candy recipes in other sections of this book which call for gelatin as an ingredient are: Christmas Cherry Fudge, Strawberry Divinity, Raspberry Pink Divinity, Jellied Centers (for chocolates), Marshmallow Easter Eggs, Creamy Walnut Taffy, Northwestern Apricot Candy and Northwestern Apple Candy. Do look them up in the Index.

## HOMEMADE MARSHMALLOWS

*Light, delicate and delicious*

2 tblsp. unflavored gelatin
¾ c. cold water
2 c. sugar
⅛ tsp. salt

¾ c. boiling water
1 tblsp. vanilla
Chopped nuts or toasted flaked
   coconut for coating

Soften gelatin in cold water 5 minutes; then dissolve by stirring over hot water.

Combine sugar, salt and boiling water in 2-qt. heavy saucepan; cook, stirring until sugar dissolves, to the soft crack stage (280°).

Pour into mixing bowl along with the gelatin mixture and beat at low speed for 3 minutes; continue beating at medium speed for 10 minutes or until mixture is fluffy and creamy. Add vanilla and pour into an 8″ square pan dusted with confectioners sugar.

Cool ½ hour or until set, then cut in 36 squares with knife moistened in water. Roll in nuts or coconut. Place in airtight container and put in refrigerator, freezer or other cold place until ready to use. Makes about 1 pound.

NOTE: Tint the gelatin mixture while heating—pale green, pink or yellow—if you wish. Roll green candy in chopped nuts, pink in flaked coconut, yellow in toasted coconut and white in nuts or coconut. You can vary the flavorings if you wish. Instead of vanilla use almond, peppermint, orange or lemon extract.

## CANDIED MARSHMALLOWS

*A children's party special that grownups also enjoy—try them*

| | |
|---|---|
| ½ c. sugar | 1 (4 oz.) pkg. marshmallows |
| ½ c. light corn syrup | (16) |
| ½ c. smooth peanut butter | |

Combine sugar and corn syrup in 1-qt. heavy saucepan. Cook over medium heat, stirring constantly, until mixture comes to a boil and sugar is dissolved.

Remove from heat; stir in peanut butter until well blended.

With 2 forks, dip marshmallows, one at a time, into mixture until evenly coated. Place on buttered cake racks, set on waxed paper, to drain and cool. Makes 16.

## CANDY STRAWBERRIES

*So sparkly, with a fresh strawberry taste*

| | |
|---|---|
| 2 (3 oz.) pkgs. strawberry flavor gelatin | ½ tsp. vanilla |
| | Red sugar crystals |
| 1 c. ground pecans | Green food color |
| 1 c. ground coconut | Slivered almonds |
| ¾ c. sweetened condensed milk | |

Mix together gelatin, pecans, coconut, condensed (not evaporated) milk and vanilla. Shape mixture into strawberries; chill at least 1 hour.

Roll chilled berries in sugar crystals.

Add food color to almonds to tint a delicate green. Use for leaves and stems of berries. Store in a cool place. Makes about 48 strawberries, depending on size, or 1 pound, 3 ounces.

# After-Dinner Jellies

Instead of gelatin, liquid fruit pectin from the supermarket shelf sets these delightful jellied confections. The orange jellies in fluted chocolate cups make such a pretty picture that guests will start exclaiming whenever the confections appear. And after they sample the fresh orange taste, you'll hear how good the jellies are.

## AFTER-DINNER JELLIES

*Fluted chocolate cups hold orange-flavored jellied candy*

½ oz. paraffin (2×1×½")
8 squares semisweet chocolate
 (8 oz. pkg.)
1 (6 oz.) bottle liquid fruit
 pectin
½ tsp. baking soda
1 c. sugar

1 c. light corn syrup
1 tsp. grated orange peel
1½ tsp. orange extract
Few drops red and yellow food
 color
3 tblsp. chopped nuts

Melt paraffin and chocolate in top of double boiler over hot (not boiling) water; stir. With a small spatula, coat insides of thirty 1½" fluted paper cups with chocolate (keep chocolate over hot water while you work). Refrigerate until firm.

Pour pectin into a 2-qt. saucepan; stir in soda. (Pectin will foam.)

Mix sugar and corn syrup in another saucepan. Place both saucepans over highest heat. Cook mixtures, stirring alternately, until foam has disappeared from pectin mixture and sugar mixture is boiling rapidly, about 3 to 5 minutes.

Pour pectin mixture in stream into boiling sugar mixture, stirring constantly. Boil and stir for 1 minute.

Remove from heat, add orange peel, extract and food color. Spoon quickly into chocolate cups. Sprinkle with nuts. Refrigerate until firm. Store in covered pan in refrigerator. Peel off papers to serve. Makes 30 jellies.

N O T E : This treat is not recommended for packing and shipping.

# Perfect Caramels

Pass a plate or box of caramels to friends and observe the anticipation in their eyes as they help themselves. Their compliments will be proof, if you need it, that caramels are a top favorite.

Contrary to hearsay, they are not difficult to make, but you can't daydream while they're cooking. The candy mixture burns easily and requires watching. The steps to perfect caramels are few and simple:

Cook caramel candy over low heat most of the time, especially during the last part of the cooking.

Stir almost constantly to prevent curdling and scorching.

Keep sides of saucepan wiped free of sugar crystals with a damp cloth-covered fork or pastry brush.

Cook candy to 246 or 248°, as you prefer, unless recipe directs otherwise. Candy cooked to 246° will be a little softer, or less firm, than that cooked to 248°.

You can add chopped nuts; but if you cut up the nuts, the caramels will be free from cloudiness (chopping produces some very fine particles or dust).

*Lightly* butter or oil pan into which you pour candy to cool. Excess butter or oil is especially noticeable on caramels.

Either turn the cool candy onto a cutting board, cut it in strips with a knife having a long, sharp blade, or cut it in strips while in pan and lift them to cutting board. Wipe off any excess butter or oil. Cut in pieces with sawing movement so candy will not stick to knife.

Wrap the pieces individually in waxed paper as soon as possible when they are cold to keep them from getting sticky. You can twist the waxed paper around a piece of candy at both ends, but so wrapped, it will not package neatly or attractively. A better, more professional-looking way: Lay the caramel on small pieces of waxed paper the right size (depends on size of caramels). Turn up two opposite sides of paper over candy to meet with no more than ¼" overlap. Then fold other ends, one at a time, in a V as you do in wrapping a parcel post package. Press these ends against candy. They should not be long enough to overlap the caramel. Or wrap pieces in aluminum foil.

Store caramels in refrigerator or other cool place.


## VANILLA CARAMELS

*Use canned condensed milk, no cream in this successful recipe*

| | |
|---|---|
| 2 c. white sugar | 1 c. milk |
| 1 c. light brown sugar | ⅓ c. butter |
| 1 c. light corn syrup | ¼ tsp. salt |
| 1 c. sweetened condensed milk | 2 tsp. vanilla |

Combine sugars, corn syrup, condensed (not evaporated) milk and milk in a 3-qt. heavy saucepan. Cook over medium heat, stirring until sugars are dissolved and syrup starts to boil. Reduce heat to low and cook, stirring occasionally to prevent scorching, until mixture reaches 240°. Cook and stir constantly to avoid scorching until mixture reaches the firm ball stage (246 to 248°).

Remove from heat; add butter and salt and stir in well. After about 2 minutes, add vanilla and stir.

Pour into a lightly buttered 8" square pan. When it starts to get firm, mark candy in ¾" strips with sharp knife. When cool and firm (about 3 hours), cut in strips; remove strips from pan, one at a time; place on cutting board and with a sharp knife, cut in squares or rectangles. Wrap individually in waxed paper. Makes 10 to 11 dozen pieces, or 2½ pounds.


## SCHOOL GIRL CARAMELS

*Include these in the box you mail to the girl away at school*

| | |
|---|---|
| 1 c. sugar | ¼ c. butter (½ stick) |
| 1 c. light corn syrup | |
| 1 c. light cream (or ½ c. heavy cream plus ½ c. milk) | |

Combine all ingredients in 2-qt. heavy saucepan. Stir over medium heat until sugar is dissolved and mixture starts to boil. Reduce heat and cook at a fairly low, steady boil, stirring occasionally until mixture reaches 240°. Then stir constantly and vigorously to prevent scorching until mixture reaches the firm ball stage (246 to 248°).

Remove from heat at once and pour into a lightly buttered 8" square pan. Let cool about 1 hour, or until candy starts to become firm. Then score in strips about ¾" wide. When cool and firm, remove strips from pan, one at a time; lay on cutting board and with a very sharp knife, cut in 9 even-sized pieces. Wrap each piece in waxed paper. Makes about 80 to 90 pieces, or 1¼ pounds.

## VERMONT CARAMELS

*Maple syrup provides flavor, sweetening—well worth using this way*

| | |
|---|---|
| 2 c. light brown sugar, firmly packed | 2 tblsp. light or dark corn syrup |
| 1½ c. maple syrup | ½ c. heavy cream |
| | 1 tblsp. butter |

Combine brown sugar, maple syrup, corn syrup and cream in a 3-qt. heavy saucepan. Stir with a wooden spoon to mix; cook over medium heat at first, then reduce heat to low as the mixture reaches 240°; stir to avoid sticking. Add butter; stir to blend well. Continue cooking, stirring constantly and vigorously to prevent scorching, to the firm ball stage (246 to 248°).

Remove from heat and pour into a lightly buttered 8" square pan. Score in ¾" strips as it hardens. Let set 3 to 4 hours. Remove candy from pan; lay on cutting board and cut in pieces. Wrap individually in waxed paper. Makes about 8 dozen, or 1½ pounds.

## Variation

**Maple Nut Caramels**   Add ½ c. coarsely chopped pecans or walnuts just before removing from heat.

## NUT CARAMELS

*This combination of nut and caramel flavors is an unbeatable one*

| | |
|---|---|
| 2 c. dairy half-and-half or light cream | ½ tsp. salt |
| 2 c. sugar | ⅓ c. butter or margarine |
| 1 c. light corn syrup | ½ c. cut-up nuts |
| | 1 tsp. vanilla |

Heat half-and-half until lukewarm in 3-qt. heavy saucepan. Pour out 1 c. and set aside. Add sugar, corn syrup and salt to cream in saucepan. Cook over medium heat, stirring constantly, until mixture boils. Slowly add remaining 1 c. half-and-half so that syrup does not stop boiling. Cook 5 minutes, stirring constantly.

Stir in butter, about 1 tsp. at a time. Turn heat to low. Boil gently (at low boil), stirring occasionally to prevent mixture sticking to pan, until it reaches the firm ball stage (246 to 248°).

Remove from heat. Gently stir in nuts and vanilla.

Let stand 10 minutes, then stir just enough to distribute the nuts. Pour into one corner of a lightly buttered 8″ square pan, letting mixture flow to its own level in pan (do not scrape cooking pan). Cool to room temperature.

Turn out onto cutting board (if candy sticks, heat bottom of pan slightly. Let candy cool before cutting). Mark off in ¾″ squares; when cool and firm, cut with large sharp knife. Wrap each piece in waxed paper or plastic wrap. Makes about 8 dozen caramels, or 2 pounds.

## SPECIAL VANILLA CARAMELS

*Compliment winners—you'll be urged to "make that candy again"!*

| | |
|---|---|
| 2 c. white sugar | 1 c. butter (2 sticks) |
| 1 c. light brown sugar | 1 c. milk |
| 1 c. light corn syrup | ½ to ⅔ c. chopped nuts |
| 1 c. light cream (or ½ c. heavy | (optional) |
| cream plus ½ c. dairy half- | 4 tsp. vanilla |
| and-half) | |

Combine all ingredients, except nuts and vanilla, in a 3-qt. heavy saucepan. Place over medium heat; stir until sugars are dissolved and butter is melted.

Reduce heat and cook, stirring occasionally (stir down any foam). When candy reaches 240° stir constantly to avoid scorching, and cook to firm ball stage (246 to 248°). Remove from heat at once, and let stand about 2 minutes.

Add nuts and vanilla; stir to mix. Pour into a lightly buttered 9″ square pan. When candy starts to get firm, mark in ¾″ strips with knife. When cool and firm (about 3 hours), cut in strips. Remove strips from pan, one at a time; place on cutting board and cut in squares or rectangles with sharp knife. Wrap individually in waxed paper. Makes about 11 dozen pieces, or 2½ pounds.

## CHOCOLATE CARAMELS

*A thoughtful gift for the holidays—candy is rich and chewy*

2½ c. white sugar
1 c. light corn syrup
1 c. water
1 c. light cream (or ½ c. heavy cream plus ½ c. dairy half-and-half)

1 c. butter (2 sticks)
3 squares unsweetened chocolate
1½ oz. piece paraffin (1½ × 1½ × ⅝" thick), cut in small pieces

Combine all ingredients in a 4-qt. heavy saucepan. Stir and cook over medium heat until sugar is dissolved and butter and paraffin melted. Reduce heat to low and cook, stirring occasionally, until mixture reaches 240°. This will take about 30 to 40 minutes. Continue to cook, stirring constantly and vigorously to prevent scorching, to the firm ball stage (248°). (The entire cooking period will be 50 to 60 minutes.)

Remove from heat at once and pour into a lightly buttered 9" square pan. When candy starts to get firm, mark in ¾" strips with a knife. When candy is cool and firm (about 3 hours), cut in strips with knife. Remove strips from pan, one at a time; place on cutting board and with sharp knife, cut in squares or rectangles. Wrap individually in waxed paper. Makes about 10 dozen caramels, or 2¼ pounds.

## Unforgettable Caramel Pecan Logs

You don't often taste homemade candy as luscious as Caramel Pecan Logs. This is one of the most praised treats our recipe testers have made. The Kansas FARM JOURNAL reader who first sent us the recipe says: "I've been making the logs for at least 15 years. They take more time than most candies, but they're worth every minute spent. I like to make the centers one day to refrigerate for cutting, dipping and rolling in nuts the next day."

Scarcely had we tested the recipe, when along came a letter from an Illinois homemaker with almost the same recipe. She wrote: "I'm eternally grateful to my sister-in-law, who gave me the recipe for Caramel Pecan Logs. Sometimes I roll the caramel-dipped logs in coconut instead of pecans. And for variety, I occasionally make chocolate nougat centers by adding 2 squares of unsweetened chocolate, melted with the butter."

Both of the champion makers of this superb candy offer the same important suggestion: Make this candy only if you have a candy thermometer.

This isn't a new recipe, but one of the tried and true treasures.

## CARAMEL PECAN LOGS

*One of the best taste treats Santa could bring anyone for Christmas —our big recipe, just right for gifts*

*Nougat Center:*

| | |
|---|---|
| 3 c. sugar | ¼ c. melted butter |
| 1⅓ c. light corn syrup | 1 tsp. vanilla |
| 1 c. water | ⅛ tsp. salt |
| 2 egg whites, stiffly beaten | |

*Caramel Coating:*

| | |
|---|---|
| 2 c. sugar | ¼ tsp. salt |
| 1¼ c. light corn syrup | 1½ lbs. pecans, coarsely |
| 1½ c. light cream | chopped (about 6 c.) |
| 1 tsp. vanilla | |

To make nougat center, combine ¾ c. sugar, ⅔ c. corn syrup and ¼ c. water in 1½-qt. heavy saucepan. Stir over medium heat until sugar dissolves; then boil to soft ball stage (238°).

Pour syrup over beaten egg whites, beating constantly until slightly cool; this takes about 5 minutes. Spoon into well-buttered bowl and make a well in the center. Let stand while you make the second syrup.

Combine remaining 2¼ c. sugar, ⅔ c. corn syrup and ¾ c. water. Cook over medium heat, stirring until sugar is dissolved. Continue cooking to the hard ball stage (258°).

Pour syrup immediately into center of egg white mixture in bowl. Beat vigorously with wooden spoon until thoroughly mixed. Stir in butter, vanilla and salt.

Let stand, beating occasionally, until mixture is very stiff and holds its shape. Transfer from bowl into waxed paper-lined 8″ square pan. With buttered fingers, press it into pan. Keep in the refrigerator until very firm—for 2 or 3 hours or days.

Turn the firm candy onto cutting board and remove waxed paper.

Cut in half and then in half again, making 4 small squares. Cut each square into 4 logs of equal size; you'll have 16 small logs. You are now ready to make the caramel coating.

To make caramel coating, combine sugar, corn syrup and ½ c. cream in 2-qt. heavy saucepan. Stir over medium heat until sugar dissolves; cook to soft ball stage (236°).

Slowly add ½ c. cream and again cook to soft ball stage (236°). Add remaining ½ c. cream and cook mixture to firm ball stage (242°); stir often as caramel mixture thickens. Remove from heat and stir in vanilla and salt.

Pour mixture into top of double boiler and set over hot water. Gently drop nougat logs, one at a time, into caramel (work quickly with two forks), coating thoroughly; hold log over caramel to drain slightly. Drop logs into shallow dish containing nuts and roll to coat. When cool, wrap logs in aluminum foil and store in refrigerator at least 5 hours, or for weeks. When ready to serve, cut in ½" slices. Makes 4¾ pounds or about 128 slices.

## HOLIDAY LOGS

*Professional-looking, easy to make; logs make a hit when shared*

| | |
|---|---|
| ⅓ c. soft butter or margarine | Red food color |
| ¼ c. light corn syrup | Few drops oil of cinnamon |
| 1 tsp. vanilla | Few drops rum extract |
| ½ tsp. salt | 1 lb. caramels (light or dark) |
| 1 lb. confectioners sugar | 3 tblsp. light cream or |
| Green food color | evaporated milk |
| Few drops of oil of peppermint | 1½ c. chopped pecans, toasted |

To make fondant center, combine butter, syrup, vanilla and salt in a large mixing bowl. Add confectioners sugar; mix together with a fork, then knead with hands. Mixture will be very dry, but softens with kneading.

Divide in thirds. Knead on board, blending green color and oil of peppermint into one third, red food color and oil of cinnamon into another third and rum extract into last third. (Adjust flavorings to taste.)

Form into rolls 1" in diameter. Cut fondant rolls in halves

crosswise to make 6 rolls. Wrap individually in waxed paper and store overnight in freezer or refrigerator.

Make caramel-nut coating next day by heating caramels and cream in double boiler. Dip chilled fondant rolls into warm caramel mixture, spooning to cover. (Work quickly so rolls don't soften.) Immediately roll in chopped pecans; wrap in aluminum foil and chill. Store logs in refrigerator or freezer until ready to serve. Slice just before serving. Makes 2⅓ pounds.

## CARAMEL APPLE SLICES

*Praline-like; spicy and sweet*

| | |
|---|---|
| 2 c. white sugar | 2 tblsp. butter or margarine |
| 1 c. brown sugar, firmly packed | ½ tsp. ground cinnamon |
| 1 c. finely grated, peeled apples | ¼ tsp. salt |
| and juice (2 medium apples) | ½ c. miniature marshmallows |
| ¾ c. evaporated milk | 1 c. chopped pecans or walnuts |

Combine first 7 ingredients in 3-qt. heavy saucepan. Cook to soft ball stage (240°). Mixture scorches easily, so stir often. Without scraping saucepan, pour into buttered 13×9×2″ pan; cool at room temperature.

When completely cooled, divide candy in half. Pat each half into an 8×6″ rectangle on waxed paper. Place double row of marshmallows along one 8″ edge. Roll as for jelly roll; roll in chopped nuts. Repeat with other rectangle of candy.

Wrap in waxed paper. Chill until firm; then cut in ¼″ slices. Store in airtight container. Makes 3 dozen ¼″ slices.

N O T E : This candy is not recommended for packing and shipping.

## CARAMEL MALLOW ROLL-UP

*Candy, marshmallows and walnuts—the young crowd likes this*

| | |
|---|---|
| ½ lb. light caramels (28) | 2 c. confectioners sugar, sifted |
| ¼ c. dairy half-and-half | 17 regular marshmallows |
| 2 tblsp. butter | ¾ c. finely chopped walnuts |

Combine caramels, half-and-half and butter in 1½-qt. heavy saucepan. Place over heat and stir until caramels are melted. Stir in confectioners sugar. Remove from heat.

Spread caramel mixture on buttered waxed paper to make a 16×5″ rectangle.

Place marshmallows, end to end, along one long side of rectangle. Roll up, starting with marshmallow side, by lifting with waxed paper. Spread nuts on waxed paper; coat roll with them. Wrap in waxed paper. Chill several hours. To serve, cut in ½″ slices. Makes 1 (16″) log, or about 32 pieces.

## CANDY TURTLES

*Spread turtles on tray—they're eye openers and make candy-talk*

| | |
|---|---|
| ½ lb. soft caramels (25) | 1¼ c. pecan halves (about) |
| 2 tblsp. heavy cream | 4 squares semisweet chocolate |

Melt caramels with cream over hot water. Let cool about 10 minutes.

Arrange pecan halves in groups of three on lightly greased baking sheet (one for head of turtle and two for legs).

Spoon melted caramels over nuts, leaving tips showing. Let stand at least 30 minutes.

Melt chocolate over hot water. Remove from water and stir until smooth. Cool; spread over caramel of turtles (do not cover nut tips). Makes 24 turtles.

# Wonderful Oklahoma Brown Candy

You'll never put more delicious candy in your mouth than Oklahoma Brown Candy. The recipe for it originated in the Sooner State, where the candy is a favorite. Its color is a rich caramel brown and it's a first cousin of caramels. The superb flavor comes from the caramelized sugar and the generous amount of pecans, a native Oklahoma nut, embedded in the luscious sweetness. You can use half the amount of pecans if you wish, or you can use other kinds of nuts. But once you take the pecans out of Oklahoma Brown Candy you must delete Oklahoma from its name.

You may want a helper standing by, at least the first time you make this candy. The trick is to get the sugar caramelized and ready to pour at the same time the sugar-milk mixture reaches the boil. Also, it's helpful to have someone share the beating.

Some Oklahoma women use their pressure cooker kettles for the saucepan in which to cook the candy. The recipe makes a big batch, so a deep cooking pan is desirable. Sometimes they pour the candy into loaf pans and, when cold, remove it from the pans, wrap the loaves in foil or plastic wrap and store them in the refrigerator to cut in slices as they wish. This candy is an excellent keeper if wrapped and refrigerated. Or you can freeze it.


## OKLAHOMA BROWN CANDY

*Let's give thanks to the Sooners who invented this superlative candy*

6 c. sugar
2 c. milk or dairy half-and-half
¼ tsp. baking soda
½ c. butter or margarine
  (1 stick)

1 tsp. vanilla
2 lbs. pecans, broken (about
  8½ c.)

Combine 4 c. sugar and milk in 4-qt. heavy saucepan. Stir and set aside.

Put remaining 2 c. sugar in 10″ heavy skillet over medium heat. Stir constantly until sugar starts to melt. Then place sugar-milk mixture over low heat, stirring occasionally until sugar dissolves.

Continue melting sugar in skillet, stirring, until all is melted and is the color of light brown sugar. (Melting sugar scorches easily so watch carefully.) This may take almost 30 minutes.

Pour melted sugar in a fine stream into the boiling sugar-milk mixture, stirring constantly. The secret to success is to pour it in a very fine stream.

Cook combined mixture to the firm ball stage (246°). Remove from heat at once. Stir in baking soda. The mixture foams vigorously when soda is added. Add butter and let stand 30 minutes.

Add vanilla and beat with wooden spoon until mixture loses its gloss and begins to thicken. Add pecans, and stir to mix.

Pour into lightly buttered 13×9×2″ pan. Cool slightly and cut in pieces of the desired size. Makes 4½ to 5 pounds.

## HAWAIIAN COFFEE CANDY

*A rich caramel flavor with faint coffee-vanilla undertones—chewy*

| | |
|---|---|
| 1 c. light corn syrup | ½ c. evaporated milk |
| 2 c. sugar | 2 tblsp. butter |
| 3 tblsp. instant coffee powder | 1 tblsp. vanilla |

Combine corn syrup, sugar, coffee powder and evaporated milk in a 2-qt. heavy saucepan. Brush sides of pan with melted butter. Bring to a boil, stirring until sugar is dissolved. Cook to soft ball stage (236 to 238°). Add 2 tblsp. butter and continue cooking to firm ball stage (242°); stir to prevent scorching. Remove from heat and cool 10 minutes.

Add vanilla (1 tblsp. is correct) and blend. Pour at once into lightly buttered 8″ square pan. When cool, with tip of knife mark in 9 strips, each about ¾″ wide. When cold and firm, cut strips; lift out one at a time and cut in squares. Place on buttered baking sheet. Wrap in plastic wrap, twisting each end. Makes about 80 pieces, or 1½ pounds.

# Try a Taffy Pull

It takes pull to make taffy, but the experience—and results—are worth the time and effort. Sharing the work and eating pleasure with family or friends on a winter day, when you want to stay indoors, gives you an understanding of how much fun the old-fashioned candy pull brought to country homes.

An Indiana mother is reviving the old custom. She writes: "My two children, 10 and 12 years, were so restless one afternoon last winter when we were snowbound, that I decided to show them how to make and pull taffy. A few weeks later they asked to invite three friends over for a Friday evening taffy pull. I helped them cook the candy and then left the kitchen. Sounds of merriment proved they liked the pulling—and tasting.

"We plan to have another taffy party. I really think our kitchen is the most cheerful and prettiest room in the house. This is a good way to entertain there."

For success with taffy, try one of the recipes that follow. If the candy should get sugary, put it in a saucepan with 2 tblsp. corn syrup and ¾ c. water. Cook it over low heat, stirring constantly until the taffy dissolves. Then cook it as the recipe directs.

## How to Pull Taffy

Turn the cooked, hot candy into a buttered shallow pan or large buttered platter. Turn the edges to the center with a heavy spatula. This encourages even cooling.

Start pulling as soon as taffy is cool enough to handle. If it gets too cool to pull easily, warm it a few minutes in a moderate oven (350°).

Pull with tips of fingers and thumbs. If candy sticks, dip fingertips in cornstarch. Some candy makers prefer to butter their fingers lightly.

Pull candy slowly until hands are about 18″ apart. Fold half of candy back on other half and continue pulling and folding until taffy gets hard to pull. (Some of our recipes indicate how taffy looks at this stage.)

Divide pulled candy in thirds or fourths; work with one part at a time. With one end of candy on a buttered surface or a surface dusted with confectioners sugar, stretch taffy to make a rope from ½ to ¾″ thick. Repeat with other portions of pulled taffy. Some candy makers prefer to twist the ropes even though the taffy is less fluffy than when untwisted. (Twisting removes the small airholes.)

Cut the ropes in bite-size pieces with buttered scissors. Cut one piece, then turn the rope of taffy halfway over and cut another piece. Continue cutting and turning.

Let pieces fall separately onto a surface that has been buttered or dusted with confectioners sugar. When cold, wrap pieces individually in waxed paper; if desired, place in airtight containers and put in freezer or refrigerator. Wrapping pieces of taffy individually in waxed paper makes it keep better, but it may be stored successfuly unwrapped in airtight containers in refrigerator or freezer.

## FOOLPROOF VANILLA TAFFY

*Both cinnamon and vanilla taffy are good. Which will you make?*

| | |
|---|---|
| 3 c. sugar | 2 tblsp. butter |
| 2 c. less 2 tblsp. light corn syrup | 1 tsp. vanilla |
| 1 c. water | |

Butter sides of a 3-qt. heavy saucepan; add sugar, corn syrup and water. Stir with a wooden spoon until sugar dissolves. Bring to a boil quickly over medium-high heat. Stir as little as possible and do not scrape sides of pan above cooking mixture (to prevent sugar crystals forming). If sugar crystals form on sides of pan, wipe them off. Cook to the hard ball stage (256°).

Add butter and continue cooking to 262°. Remove from heat. Pour into buttered and chilled shallow pan or platter (about 13×9″); turn edges to center with heavy spatula. While candy cools, make several gashes on surface; add vanilla (to be worked in during pulling).

When candy is cool enough to handle, pull until taffy changes to a shiny platinum ribbon (see directions for How to Pull Taffy).

Cut in bite-size pieces with buttered scissors. Cool, then wrap pieces individually in waxed paper. Store in airtight containers. Makes 2½ pounds.

## Variation

**Cinnamon Taffy** Instead of vanilla, add 6 to 8 drops oil of cinnamon while taffy is cooling, kneading candy with a spatula at first, then with hands before dividing and pulling.

## CREAMY WALNUT TAFFY

*Gelatin and cream are the unusual ingredients in this new taffy. It gets creamy and improves as it stands*

| | |
|---|---|
| ½ tsp. unflavored gelatin | 1 c. light corn syrup |
| ¼ c. cold water | 2 tsp. melted paraffin |
| 2 c. sugar | ¼ tsp. baking soda |
| 1 c. light cream (or ½ c. heavy cream plus ½ c. dairy half-and-half) | ½ c. finely chopped walnuts |
| | 1 tsp. vanilla |

Soften gelatin in cold water.

Combine sugar, cream, corn syrup, paraffin and softened gelatin in 2-qt. heavy saucepan; stir to dissolve sugar. Quickly bring to a boil over medium-high heat and cook, stirring as little as possible, to the hard ball stage (256°). Continue cooking to 262°.

Remove from heat; add soda, nuts and vanilla, and stir to combine. Pour into buttered shallow pan or platter (about 13×9″). Turn edges to center with heavy spatula.

When candy is cool enough to handle, pull until taffy takes on an opaque look (see directions for How to Pull Taffy). Cut in bite-size pieces with buttered scissors. Cool, then wrap pieces individually in waxed paper; store in airtight containers. Makes 2 pounds.

## OLD-FASHIONED MOLASSES TAFFY

*Reminds grandparents of taffy-pulling fun on wintry evenings*

| | |
|---|---|
| 2 c. molasses | 2 tblsp. butter |
| 1 c. sugar | 1 tblsp. vinegar |

Combine ingredients in a 3-qt. heavy saucepan. Stir with a

wooden spoon until sugar is dissolved; bring to a boil over medium heat. If mixture foams during cooking, stir around the outside under the cooking surface and if excessive, reduce heat to medium-low. Continue to cook to the hard ball stage (260°).

Pour taffy into a large (about 13×9″) buttered and chilled shallow pan or platter (do not scrape cooking pan). Turn edges to center with heavy spatula.

When candy is cool enough to handle, pull until taffy is light in color and hard to pull (see directions for How to Pull Taffy). Cut in bite-size pieces with buttered scissors. Cool, then wrap pieces individually in waxed paper; store in airtight containers. Makes 1¾ pounds.

## Variation

**Peppermint Molasses Taffy** While taffy is cooling, add 4 to 5 drops oil of peppermint; work it into the candy as you pull. Candy has a delicious flavor.

### PEPPERMINT TAFFY STICKS

*The pink of perfection in taffy*

| | |
|---|---|
| 2 c. sugar | 5 drops red food color |
| ½ c. light corn syrup | ¼ tsp. oil of peppermint |
| ⅔ c. water | |

Combine sugar, corn syrup and water in 2-qt. heavy saucepan. Stir over low heat until sugar is dissolved. Add food color to tint a delicate pink and cook without stirring to the hard ball stage (265°).

Remove from heat and add oil of peppermint.

Pour into buttered shallow pan (about 13×9″) or onto buttered platter. When cool enough to handle, pull until light and fluffy (see directions for How to Pull Taffy). Quickly stretch in thin ropes and twist around oiled 4½″ wooden lollipop sticks (from meat counter). When set, slip taffy from sticks and wrap coils individually in waxed paper. Place in airtight container and store in a cool place. To serve, remove waxed paper wrappings. Makes about 1¼ pounds.

NOTE: You can stretch part or all of pulled taffy into ropes and cut in pieces as with any taffy. Wrap each piece in waxed paper, twisting paper ends.

## SALT WATER TAFFY

*You can divide taffy, tinting and flavoring each portion differently*

| | |
|---|---|
| 2 c. sugar | 2 tsp. glycerin |
| 1 c. light corn syrup | 2 tblsp. butter |
| 1½ c. water | 2 tsp. vanilla |
| 1½ tsp. salt | |

Combine sugar, syrup, water, salt and glycerin in a 3-qt. heavy saucepan. Place on low heat and stir until sugar dissolves. Then cook without stirring to the hard ball stage (260°).

Remove from heat and add butter. When butter is melted, pour into a buttered shallow pan (about 13×9″).

When cool enough to handle, gather into a ball and pull until rather firm. Add vanilla while pulling. Stretch out into a long rope and cut in 1 or 2″ pieces. Wrap each piece in waxed paper when hard; twist paper at both ends. This will keep candy from becoming sticky. Makes about 1¼ pounds.

N O T E : You can tint the taffy while pulling it. Different flavors may be added, also in the pulling, instead of the vanilla. Pink taffy usually is flavored with wintergreen, white with vanilla, green with spearmint.

## PULLED MINTS

*You pull this like taffy, getting mints that melt in your mouth*

| | |
|---|---|
| 2 c. sugar | Few drops food color (your |
| 1 c. water | choice) |
| ¼ c. butter or margarine | 4 to 5 drops oil of peppermint |
| (½ stick) | or wintergreen, lemon or |
| Pinch cream of tartar | cinnamon |

Combine sugar, water, butter and cream of tartar in 2-qt. heavy saucepan. Stir over medium heat until sugar is completely dissolved.

Cook, without stirring, over high heat until mixture reaches the hard ball stage (260°). If sugar crystals form on sides of pan, wipe them off.

Pour onto buttered marble slab or buttered large shallow pan or platter. With buttered hands, turn edges into center so they won't get hard. Let cool.

When cool enough to handle, sprinkle over drops of food color and your choice of flavor. Pick up into a ball. Hold in one hand, pull out with other hand; fold back and pull again, working in color and flavoring (see directions for How to Pull Taffy). Turn, to pull all parts evenly. Continue pulling until almost cold.

Stretch out in a "ribbon" of even thickness (about ½" to ¾" wide). Cut off with kitchen shears in short lengths. Store in airtight container with waxed paper between layers. Makes about 1 pound.

# Hard Candies
## Crystal-Clear and Color-Bright

When the weather-watcher in the country family steps outdoors to look at the sky before retiring and comes in predicting a fair, dry tomorrow, candy makers take notice; especially if you want to make hard candies, since they have a remarkable affinity for water—absorb it from the air and quickly become sticky. The first step to success in making hard candy is choosing a fair day low in humidity.

You want hard candies crystal-clear and color-bright. So you have to try to prevent sugar crystals from forming; they affect both clearness and color. Here are ways to avoid crystallization:

Include corn syrup with the sugar and liquid in the saucepan —that is, choose a recipe that contains the syrup. Ours do!

When you put it on to cook, stir the candy mixture until the sugar dissolves; then refrain from stirring during the remainder of the cooking. Keep it at a steady, fairly low boil.

Remove any sugar crystals that form by wiping sides of saucepan with a damp, cloth-covered fork or pastry brush.

The cooking syrup tends to darken toward the end of the cooking. This dulls the color when you tint the candy. One way to prevent darkening is to cook the candy in a saucepan with deep, straight sides so there is a relatively small cooking surface. In some of our tests we used the top of a large double boiler, which is ideal in shape (rounded bottom) and size. It also helps, when the temperature reaches 280°, to lower the heat for the remainder of the cooking.

Add the flavoring and food color as soon as the candy is cooked, first removing it from the heat. Oil flavorings are desirable because they are strong. You may think you are adding a lot, but some of the flavor "goes up in smoke," or evaporates. That's what gives the kitchen such an enchanting aroma. Paste food color is a favorite for hard candies. You dissolve it in very little water before adding it to the candy. Stir the coloring and flavoring into the candy just enough to mix. Too much stirring may produce sugar crystals.

These candies deserve their name because they harden quickly. You have to work fast once the cooking ends. If you pour the candy into an oiled pan to cool, stand by to mark it in pieces just as soon as it cools enough to hold an impression. The candy will still feel warm. Score the candy in strips, first one direction, then across, to mark it in pieces. Use a sharp, strong knife, working the knife back and forth to make an impression—but do not cut through the candy.

When the candy is cold, turn the pan over on counter top or cutting board and give it a tap. The candy will fall out. Break it in pieces along the lines made with the knife. Store candy in airtight containers with waxed paper between the layers, or wrap each piece individually in waxed paper or plastic wrap. Put in a cool place. Unless the pieces are individually wrapped, don't box hard candy with other kinds of candy. (Hard candies rob other candies of their moisture—the hard candies will become sticky and the other ones will dry out.)

## Fascinating Lollypops

Lollypops shaped like roosters, squirrels and deer got a Michigan mother involved in the candy business. She took some of the lollypops she makes for her seven children to a food bazaar. They not only sold quickly, but people telephoned her and came to her door asking her to make and sell animal lollypops for them to give to their children and grandchildren. The pleas were so sincere that she yielded and now, every year starting at Halloween and continuing up to the Christmas holidays, she makes and sells lollypops.

She shapes them with heavy, cast metal molds. These are not easily found and are rather expensive (but a good investment for her). An imaginative mother in the West, unable to find molds, substitutes cookie cutters *open* at both top and bottom. A good way to display lollypops at a food sale is to insert the stick ends in a large circle of Styrofoam.

Increase the amount of oil flavorings if you like a more pronounced flavor. The smaller children on our taste panel preferred ⅛ tsp. oil of peppermint, for instance, while adults liked ¼ tsp. And do use different flavors and food colors. Here are a few suggestions: oil of lime or spearmint with green food color, oil of wintergreen with pink, oil of lemon with yellow, oil of orange with orange, and oil of peppermint or oil of cinnamon with red.

## LOLLYPOPS

*Children do talk to the animals when they're candy on sticks*

| | |
|---|---|
| 2 c. sugar | ⅛ tsp. salt |
| ⅔ c. light corn syrup | ⅛ tsp. oil of peppermint |
| 1 c. water | ¼ tsp. red food color |

Oil inside of small cookie cutters that are open at both top and bottom; select cutters in the shape of animals, such as a chicken, rabbit, squirrel or other animals children like, or in the shape of a Christmas tree or star, etc. Place about 4″ apart on oiled baking sheets or oiled aluminum foil.

Combine sugar, corn syrup, water and salt in 2-qt. heavy saucepan. Place over medium heat, stirring constantly until sugar dissolves and mixture comes to a boil. If sugar crystals form on sides of pan, wipe them off.

Reduce heat and cook at a steady, fairly low boil without stirring until candy mixture reaches the hard crack stage (310°).

Remove from heat; add oil of peppermint and food color. Stir only enough to mix.

Quickly pour hot candy mixture, without scraping pan, into cookie cutters. Candy should be about ¼″ thick. As soon as candy is set and while still warm, remove cutters and twist a lollypop stick (wooden meat skewer) into each candy. With broad spatula, loosen lollypops from baking sheet before they cool.

Repeat until all candy syrup is used. If it gets too hard to pour, stir over low heat just enough to melt candy. Work fast.

Wrap individually in waxed paper as soon as cool to prevent candy from absorbing moisture and becoming sticky. Store in airtight boxes. Makes about 30 lollypops, depending on size of cookie cutters used.

## Variations

**Lollypop Faces** Instead of pouring cooked lollypop mixture into cookie cutters, drop it from tip of teaspoon or tablespoon, depending on size of lollypops desired. Drop each spoonful over one end of a lollypop stick on oiled baking sheet. (Arrange sticks 4 or 5" apart on baking sheet before starting to cook candy.) When cool, outline a face and features on each lollypop by piping on confectioners sugar frosting (confectioners sugar and water), tinted if you like. Makes about 15 to 20 large lollypops.

**Halloween Lollypops** Drop hot lollypop mixture in circles or disks onto sticks as for Lollypop Faces. Press candy corn in any design desired on lollypops before they cool; they'll not adhere if candy gets too cool.

**Hard Candy Squares** Prepare candy as for Lollypops, but pour it immediately when it reaches 310° into a greased or oiled 8" square pan. Cool just until surface of candy will hold an impression. Then mark with sharp pointed knife into squares; mark lengthwise, let set a few minutes, then mark crosswise. When candy is cold, turn pan upside down over board or table top. Tap pan sharply to remove candy. Break pieces apart. Makes 64 pieces.

## ANISE CANDY

*Candy is a clear, sparkling red—attractive served on milk glass*

| | |
|---|---|
| 2 c. sugar | ¼ tsp. red food color |
| 1 c. light corn syrup | 1 tsp. oil of anise |
| ½ c. water | |

Combine sugar, corn syrup and water in 2-qt. heavy saucepan. Stir well and cook over low heat, stirring until sugar dissolves.

Continue cooking at a fairly low boil, without stirring, to the soft crack stage (280°). If sugar crystals form on sides of pan, wipe them off. (Cook slowly during the last few minutes to avoid darkening of candy syrup.)

Remove from heat; add food color and oil of anise, stirring no more than necessary to mix.

Pour into an oiled 13×9×2" pan. Candy should be in a thin layer. As it starts to cool, mark with knife in bite-size pieces. Keep scoring pieces with knife until they hold their shape.

Cool completely; remove from pan and wipe any excess oil from block of candy. Break in pieces. Place in airtight container with waxed paper between layers and store in a cool place. Makes about 130 pieces or 1½ pounds.

## Colorful Old-Fashioned Hard Candy

Fill a fancy glass or apothecary jar with peppermint-flavored Old-Fashioned Hard Candy, tinted green, and a twin container with cinnamon-flavored candy, tinted red. You'll have a sweet Christmas gift the older generation especially enjoys. Or fill little plastic bags with the candy in different colors and flavors for the holiday bazaar. "I've taken this candy in small plastic bags to food sales," says the California woman who shares her recipe. "It sells well," she adds, "especially to people who bought it at previous sales." In other words, demand increases when customers get acquainted with the candy.

The trick in making this candy is to cut it while warm. This is what the contributor of the recipe says: "I keep a pair of white cotton gloves on hand to wear when I make this candy. They make it possible for me to start cutting sooner (I learned by experience). At first I decided to let the candy cool and then break it into pieces. It looked like broken glass and no one wanted to eat it. The ideal situation is for one person to cut the candy in strips and another to snip it with scissors into pieces, because it hardens fast."

Here's another tip from the California candy maker: "I keep a saucepan partly filled with hot water on the range. If the candy be-

*CENTERPIECE YOU CAN EAT—Wreath is molded of candy-coated corn flakes (or make tiny wreaths—recipe, page 203). For gifts, offer a gold-lined box of elegant Napoleon Cremes, page 213, or a bright basketful of fresh-tasting Candy Strawberries, page 137.*

gins to cool faster than I can cut it, I set the pan of candy over the saucepan of hot water. If the candy starts to get sticky, I move it back to the work counter."

You can buy the oil flavorings at drugstores, but tell the druggist you want to use them in cooking.

## OLD-FASHIONED HARD CANDY

*Here's a slow-eating, colorful gift—pleases Grandpa and grandkids*

2 c. sugar
1 c. water
¾ c. light corn syrup
Food color (red, green, yellow, etc.)

½ tsp. oil of cinnamon, clove, peppermint, wintergreen or anise
Confectioners sugar

Combine sugar, water and corn syrup in 2-qt. heavy saucepan. Cook, stirring constantly until sugar is dissolved; then cook without stirring, lowering heat and cooking more slowly during the last few minutes, to the hard crack stage (300°). If sugar crystals form on sides of pan, wipe them off.

Remove from heat; add food color and oil flavoring, stirring only enough to mix. Pour into 2 well-buttered 9″ pie pans. Set one pan of candy over a saucepan containing hot water. As soon as the other pan of candy is cool enough to touch, cut it with scissors into strips 1″ wide, then snip strips into pieces. Work fast. Drop pieces onto a buttered baking sheet. If candy cools too quickly, set it on saucepan over hot water to soften it, but if it gets sticky, return at once to work counter. Repeat with second pan of candy.

When candy is cool, sprinkle with confectioners sugar. Store in airtight containers with waxed paper between the layers. Makes about 100 pieces or 1¼ pounds.

## "STAINED GLASS" HARD CANDY

*Use these candies to trim the tree, decorate a doorway or window*

5 or 6 foil molds
2 c. sugar
⅓ c. light corn syrup
⅓ c. water

2 tblsp. vinegar
Few drops oil of peppermint
Food color

Cut aluminum foil in shapes of stars, bells and trees. Grease foil lightly with salad oil. Fold up edges to make ½″ sides. Seal corners with freezer tape to prevent leaks.

Combine sugar, syrup, water and vinegar in 2-qt. heavy saucepan. Cook, stirring constantly until sugar is dissolved; then cook without stirring, to the hard crack stage (300°). Remove from heat, stir in flavoring and color; cool *slightly*.

Pour colored candy into molds, about ⅛″ deep; spoon to cover bottom. When candy begins to set (before it hardens) use skewer to make holes for hanging. Allow candy to harden thoroughly; remove foil. Thread with ribbon or cord to hang. (Or you may pour the candy onto greased cookie sheet to make free-form shapes.) If candy becomes too firm to pour and shape, remelt over low heat (do not boil).

**Tips:** Try unusual combinations: Swirl food color through uncolored candy with a toothpick just after pouring it into molds; make molded candies of one color and dribble with a second color to get an elegant "stained glass" effect. Make small candies for hanging on a Christmas tree, larger ones for other decorations. Cover candy ornaments with plastic wrap and store in covered container at room temperature in a *dry* place; keep flat to prevent warping.

# Other Hard Candies

Not all hard candies are clear. Three delicious examples with deeper color are Peppermint Drops with Chocolate, Swedish Hard Candy and Swedish Toffee. Once you taste these treats, it's easy to understand why they are popular in Sweden. If you want to make candy that is different and distinctive, do try the recipes. You'll reap compliments on the candies and will have requests for recipes to use in making them.

## PEPPERMINT DROPS WITH CHOCOLATE

*Tiny snowdrop peppermint candies wear chocolate topknots*

| | |
|---|---|
| 1⅓ c. sugar | 2 drops oil of peppermint |
| ½ c. water | 2 squares semisweet chocolate |
| 1 tsp. glycerin | |

Combine sugar and water in 2-qt. heavy saucepan. Cook slowly, stirring constantly, until sugar is dissolved. When sugar is dissolved, remove spoon and do not stir again. Cook until candy reaches a boil, then blend in glycerin. Cover saucepan for 3 minutes. Uncover and cook at a fairly low boil to the soft ball stage (240°).

Remove from heat. Add oil of peppermint, stirring no more than necessary to mix. Pour onto oiled baking sheet. Work with oiled knife or spatula (as for fondant [see Index]) until candy is smooth and creamy.

Roll quickly into ¾″ balls; flatten with knife. Place on oiled baking sheet.

Melt chocolate and drop on top center of peppermint candies. Makes 32 candies, or ½ pound.

## SWEDISH HARD CANDY

*This brittle, hard candy has a rich, delicious caramel-almond flavor*

1 c. sugar
1 c. dark corn syrup
⅓ c. butter

1 c. dairy half-and-half
1 c. chopped blanched almonds

Combine sugar, corn syrup, butter and dairy half-and-half in 2-qt. heavy saucepan. Cook over low heat, stirring until sugar dissolves. (Watch carefully for mixture rises high in saucepan.) Continue cooking, stirring occasionally, to the hard ball stage (250°).

Remove from heat; add chopped almonds. Pour into small fluted paper dessert cups (1½″ in diameter at bottom), or drop from teaspoon onto waxed paper to make patties. Makes 54 to 60 patties, depending on size, or 1½ pounds.

NOTE: If you remove candy from paper cups, the patties will have fluted edges.

## SWEDISH TOFFEE

*This is different from our toffees—it's hard with a chocolate flavor*

2½ c. sugar
1½ c. dark corn syrup
¼ c. cocoa
1 c. heavy cream

1 c. dairy half-and-half
6 tblsp. butter
1½ tsp. vanilla

Combine sugar, corn syrup, cocoa, cream, dairy half-and-half and 3 tblsp. butter in 3-qt. heavy saucepan. Cook over low heat, stirring until sugar dissolves. Continue cooking, stirring no more than necessary, to the hard ball stage (250°). Watch carefully, for mixture may boil to the top of saucepan.

Remove from heat; stir in remaining 3 tblsp. butter and vanilla. Pour into buttered 9" square pan to cool.

While still warm, mark in 1" squares; when cool, cut with a sharp knife and wrap individually in waxed paper. Makes 81 squares, or 2 pounds.

# No-Cook Candies

There are some excellent candies that do not require cooking. In this section, we present several favorites. You'll note that a few of them call for melting chocolate in the top of a double boiler, or warming nuts in the oven or, in the recipe for our own homemade Almond Paste, the cooking of the flour-milk mixture. But beyond that, the mixtures are not cooked. And the candies that result are delicious, even spectacular! You'll find some party specials among the recipes that follow.

There are a number of no-cook recipes for fudge in this book, too: Double Boiler Fudge, Cream Cheese Fudge, White Almond Fudge and Cheddar Cheese Fudge. Also No-Cook Divinity and No-Cook Fruit Balls. You'll find them all listed in the Index.

## Almond Wreath for Happy Occasions

If you're looking for a different, delicious and beautiful sweet to serve to guests or to carry to special friends for a holiday gift, end your search. Make an Almond Wreath. We imported the recipe for it from a Swedish home economist now living in Holland. Our taste panel actually raved about the way this candy looks and tastes.

European women can buy almond paste to make this and other candies and confections. It's not available in very many of our markets; however, you'll find this homemade version easy to make and it costs much less than the commercial kind. You can adjust the amount of almond extract to suit your taste. Some people think ½ tsp. is just right, while others prefer the candy flavored with 1 tsp. of the extract.

You can decorate the chocolate-coated wreath as elaborately or as simply as your time and inclination dictate. We scattered some of the nuts and candied cherries we had on hand over it and everyone who saw the wreath spoke of how pretty it was.

The compliments continued when we cut the candy—each slice showed its pale pink, delicate green and soft chocolate sections. The flavor blend is superb. If you want to make a showy production, do the slicing with guests looking on, eagerly anticipating a chance to eat the candy.

Be sure also to make Orange/Chocolate Roll, a variation of Almond Wreath. The light chocolate-brown center surrounds a cream-colored orange candy. You coat the candy roll with chocolate. This sweet also is an adventure in good eating.

## ALMOND PASTE

*This is the basic ingredient in three recipes that follow*

½ c. flour
⅔ c. dairy half-and-half
¾ c. (about) blanched almonds
  (¼ lb.)

½ to 1 tsp. almond extract
1 lb. confectioners sugar (about)

In 1-qt. heavy saucepan, beat flour into dairy half-and-half. Place over medium heat, beating constantly with spoon until mixture gathers in one big lump. Remove from heat and scrape mixture onto a large cutting board. Work with table knife to keep it smooth while it cools.

In the meantime, grind almonds. You will have 1 cup.

When dough is cold, work in almonds and almond extract. In the beginning, it is easiest to work with a knife, but later, put it in bowl and mix with the hands, kneading it like dough. Work in enough confectioners sugar to make a mixture that is smooth and does not stick. The amount of confectioners sugar needed varies with the weather, but work mixture, adding sugar, until it can be handled and rolled with ease. You may need a little more than 1 lb. confectioners sugar. Makes 1½ pounds.

## ALMOND WREATH

*For a high point in feasting serve this candy at a holiday open house*

1 recipe Almond Paste
1 tsp. cocoa
¼ c. finely chopped walnuts
1 drop red food color
1 tblsp. finely chopped candied
cherries
1 drop green food color

2 tblsp. finely chopped
pistachio nuts
5 squares semisweet chocolate,
melted
Decorations for wreath (nuts,
candied cherries, etc.)

Divide Almond Paste in 3 equal parts.

To one part, add cocoa to make a light brown; work in walnuts. Roll out to make a rope about 20″ long and ¾″ in diameter.

Add red food color to tint the second part a light pink. Work in finely chopped candied cherries. Roll to make a rope about ¾″ in diameter.

Add green food color to tint the third part a pale green and work in pistachio nuts. Roll to make a rope the same size as first two parts.

Place first two rolls side by side on waxed paper and brush sides where they touch with melted chocolate to hold them together. Place green part on top over place where the first and second parts join. Shape gently in circle to make a wreath.

Spread wreath with remaining melted chocolate to cover completely. Decorate with additional walnuts and candied cherries, or as desired. Makes wreath with a diameter about 8½″.

Let cool. To serve, cut in thin slices. Makes 2 pounds.

## *Variation*

**Orange/Chocolate Roll**  Divide 1 recipe Almond Paste in half. Tint one half with 1 tsp. cocoa and work in ⅓ c. chopped walnuts. Shape into a roll about 1″ in diameter, 15½″ long. Add a little confectioners sugar if necessary to prevent sticking when shaping roll.

Work 1 tsp. finely grated orange peel into second half of Almond Paste. Flatten it by rolling with rolling pin, using confectioners sugar to prevent sticking, to make a narrow piece. Place chocolate roll on top of orange strip. Then roll orange candy around the chocolate candy, sealing it by pressing seam gently with fingers. Spread with 5 squares semisweet chocolate, melted, and garnish with chopped nuts. To serve, cut in thin slices. Makes 1 roll, about 1½" in diameter and 17½ to 18" long, or 2 pounds.

# Party-Time Dutch Treats

Once you've made Almond Paste (for an Almond Wreath) and found out how easy it is to fix, how good it tastes and how inexpensive it is, you'll want to fix these handsome Dutch Treats. On a tray at a tea party or open house, they'll steal the show. They're real beauties—and so delectable.

The confections are actually nut macaroons topped with balls of Almond Paste and shiny Fondant Frosting, delicately tinted. You need not add other decorations, but silver dragées and chopped candied cherries give them a holiday look. You and your guests will be grateful for our neighbors in Holland who invented Dutch Treats.

## DUTCH TREATS

*Nut macaroons look like wee hats with brown brims; shiny pastel crowns are Fondant Frosting over Almond Paste*

1 egg, separated  
½ c. sugar  
¾ c. ground pecans  
Fondant Frosting  
½ recipe Almond Paste (see Index)

Decorations (silver dragées, chopped candied cherries, nuts, etc.)

Combine egg yolk and sugar in small mixing bowl; beat until well blended. Stir in pecans and chill until mixture is slightly firm.

Beat egg white until it holds stiff, but not dry peaks. Fold into pecan mixture.

Drop mixture from teaspoon onto greased and lightly floured baking sheet. (Confections should be very small, about the size of a cherry.)

Bake in preheated slow oven (325°) 8 to 12 minutes, or until lightly browned. Remove from baking sheet and cool on wire racks.

Drop a little Fondant Frosting on centers of cool confections, making half of them green, the other half pink. Place a small ball (size of a cranberry) of Almond Paste on top of each confection.

Dribble on Fondant Frosting to cover Almond Paste balls. Garnish green-frosted confections with silver dragées and pink-frosted ones with finely chopped candied cherries. Makes 45 to 50 confections, or about 1 pound.

## FONDANT FROSTING

*It's a glassy-like fondant candy*

1 c. plus 6 tblsp. sugar
Dash salt
⅛ tsp. cream of tartar
¾ c. water
1½ to 1¾ c. sifted
    confectioners sugar

¼ tsp. vanilla
2 to 3 drops red food color
2 to 3 drops green food color

Combine sugar, salt, cream of tartar and water in 1-qt. heavy saucepan. Cook over low heat, stirring constantly until sugar is dissolved. Then raise heat slightly and cook to 225° on candy thermometer. Remove from heat and cool to lukewarm (110°).

Place saucepan of frosting in pan of warm water and beat in confectioners sugar with wooden spoon. Add vanilla and continue to beat, adding confectioners sugar until frosting is thick and coats a metal spoon.

Remove half of frosting to bowl and tint a delicate pink with red food color. Tint remaining half of frosting with green food color.

Set saucepan and bowl of frosting in warm water so frosting will not get too thick. (If it gets too thick, add a few drops of warm water.) Dribble pink frosting over half of Dutch Treats, green frosting over remaining treats.

NOTE: To leftover Almond Paste, add ½ tsp. cocoa and 2 tblsp. finely chopped walnuts. Shape in ovals for a delicious candy. Or if you prefer, add ¼ tsp. grated orange peel to leftover Almond Paste and shape in ovals, or as desired. In Holland, where Dutch Treats rate highly, ground filberts or hazel nuts are used instead of ground pecans.

# Decorative Party Treat Candy

Let imagination be your guide when you make pretty No-Cook Party Treat candy, but select the right kind of weather. Start with a fair day with low humidity. When it's humid the candies are slow to dry.

Mold the pieces in your hands to whatever shape you like, or go fancy and put the kneaded candy through your pastry tube or cookie press.

Vary the flavorings. The almond and vanilla extract combination is just one suggestion.

Tint the candy as you like, but in subtle shades. We divided the candy in half, tinted one part pale pink, the other green. You can make your own distinctive colors by blending drops of two or more food colors—red and yellow, for instance. Or leave the candy white.

Decorate the shaped candies if you wish. Roll them in flaked coconut, chopped nuts or grated chocolate. Or dip them in melted semisweet chocolate or confection coating (see Dipping Chocolates in Index).

Make the candies at least a day or two before the party. This allows ample time for them to set and frees you from bothering with them on party day.

## NO-COOK PARTY TREAT

*The big surprise is that this fancy candy is so easy to make*

| | |
|---|---|
| 1 egg white | 1 lb. confectioners sugar |
| 2 tsp. dairy half-and-half | ¼ c. buttter or margarine |
| ⅛ tsp. almond extract | (½ stick), melted |
| 1 tsp. vanilla | 2 drops food color |
| ¼ tsp. salt | |

Combine egg white, half-and-half, almond extract and vanilla in small mixing bowl. Stir salt and half the sugar into mixture. Add butter and food color. Gradually stir in remaining sugar until the desired consistency is reached.

Knead until smooth. Mold into desired shapes. Place on waxed paper and let dry. Store in airtight container in refrigerator or freezer. Makes about 1 pound.

## OPEN HOUSE MINTS

*Ideal mints for holiday entertaining, wedding receptions, parties*

| | |
|---|---|
| 2 tblsp. butter | ⅛ tsp. oil of cinnamon |
| 2 tblsp. vegetable shortening | 2 drops green food color |
| 3 tblsp. warm water | ⅛ tsp. oil of peppermint |
| 5 c. sifted confectioners sugar | 2 drops yellow food color |
| 2 drops red food color | ⅛ tsp. oil of lemon |
| 3 tsp. warm water | |

Combine butter, shortening, 2 tblsp. warm water and 2 c. confectioners sugar. Mix thoroughly.

Add remaining 3 c. confectioners sugar and 1 tblsp. warm water (if necessary, add 1 or more tblsp. confectioners sugar to make mixture stiff enough to roll out).

Divide mixture in thirds. To one third add red food color, mixed with 1 tsp. warm water and oil of cinnamon; knead thoroughly to mix. Roll out to ⅛″ thickness on waxed paper dusted with confectioners sugar.

To another third of candy, add green food color mixed with 1 tsp. warm water and oil of peppermint. Knead to mix; roll out.

To final third of candy, add yellow food color mixed with 1 tsp. warm water and oil of lemon. Knead to mix; roll out.

Cut with very small cutters—hors d'oeuvre cutters with fancy shapes, if available, or use the inside of a doughnut cutter. Let the mints stand, bottom side up, on waxed paper at least 2 hours before placing in airtight containers. Makes about 130 mints, or 1¼ pounds.


## CHRISTMAS RIBBONS

*Three-layer candy looks like striped ribbon when sliced for servings*

| | |
|---|---|
| 4½ c. sifted confectioners sugar | 1 square unsweetened chocolate, |
| ¼ c. melted butter or margarine | melted |
| Few grains salt | ⅓ c. chopped nuts |
| 1 tsp. vanilla | Green food color |
| 2 tblsp. (about) dairy half-and-half | 2 tblsp. chopped, drained maraschino cherries |

Combine 4¼ c. confectioners sugar, butter, salt and vanilla. Add enough half-and-half to make a mixture that holds its shape. Knead until smooth. Divide in thirds.

To one third add melted chocolate. To another third add nuts and a few drops of green food color to tint a delicate green. To the last third add chopped cherries and the remaining ¼ c. confectioners sugar. Mix each portion well.

Line an 11×4″ ice cube tray with aluminum foil. Spread and pat chocolate candy evenly in bottom of tray. Place the green candy on top, spreading and patting to make an even cover over chocolate layer. Then evenly spread candy with cherries on top. Place in refrigerator at least 1 hour. Remove from tray and slice. Makes about 1¼ pounds.

N O T E : If you do not plan to use candy at once, wrap the loaf in foil and store it in freezer or refrigerator. It will stay fresh and delicious for many weeks.

## CHOCOLATE NUT ROLL

*Hungry for candy but don't want to cook? Here's your recipe*

| | |
|---|---|
| 1 square unsweetened chocolate | ½ tsp. vanilla or rum extract |
| 1 egg white | ½ c. finely chopped pecans or |
| ⅛ tsp. salt | walnuts |
| 1½ to 2 c. sifted confectioners | ½ c. coarsely chopped pecans |
| sugar | or walnuts |
| 1 tblsp. soft butter | |

Melt chocolate in 1-qt. mixing bowl over hot water. Cool slightly.

In another bowl beat egg white with salt until stiff but not dry. Gradually add 1 c. confectioners sugar together with butter and vanilla. When well mixed, add to slightly cooled chocolate and blend.

Add remaining sugar, ¼ c. at a time, enough to make a stiff mixture. Mix sugar in thoroughly. Add finely chopped nuts just before the last addition of sugar, working them through the mixture.

Cut 2 (12×6″) strips aluminum foil; place half of coarsely chopped nuts in center of each.

Form chocolate mixture into a ball; sprinkle lightly with confectioners sugar to prevent sticking to hands. Divide in half; form each half into a 6″ roll. Place each roll on nuts and continue rolling, distributing nuts to cover entire roll, until it is 1″ in diameter and 9″ long. Roll up in the foil and place in refrigerator or freezer. Let stand several hours before using. Keeps indefinitely in freezer. Cut in ½ to ¾″ slices to serve. Makes 24 (¾″) or 36 (½″) pieces, or ¾ pound.

## HONEY/PEANUT ROLLS

*A good keeper—if you hide it*

| | |
|---|---|
| 1 c. nonfat dry milk powder | ½ tsp. vanilla |
| 1 c. smooth or crunchy peanut butter | ½ tsp. rum extract or vanilla |
| 1 c. honey | ½ c. chopped peanuts (optional) |

Combine dry milk powder, peanut butter, honey and flavorings in a 2-qt. mixing bowl. Mix thoroughly; divide in half. Shape each half into a ball; cover and place in refrigerator 1 hour.

Line two 12″ strips of aluminum foil with waxed paper; sprinkle each with ¼ c. peanuts. With buttered palms of hands, shape each ball of candy into a roll 5 to 6″ long. Place each roll on peanuts and continue to roll, distributing nuts evenly. Roll from center to both ends until roll is ¾″ to 1″ in diameter. Wrap in foil and twist ends tightly. Chill thoroughly, then slice in bite-size pieces. Makes about 3 dozen pieces, or 1½ pounds.

N O T E : You can also roll candy into bite-size balls and dust lightly with confectioners sugar. Makes about 36 balls.

## CHRISTMAS CHOCOLATE BALLS

*These confections taste like candy bars—serve on plate with cookies*

| | |
|---|---|
| 1 c. smooth peanut butter | 1 tblsp. soft butter |
| 1 (8 oz.) pkg. pitted dates, cut fine (1 c.) | 1 (6 oz.) pkg. chocolate chips |
| 1 c. sifted confectioners sugar | 2 squares semisweet chocolate |
| 1 c. finely chopped nuts | 1 (1″) square paraffin wax |

Combine peanut butter, dates, sugar, nuts and butter in bowl and mix thoroughly. Shape in 1″ balls and place in refrigerator while preparing the chocolate for coating.

Melt chocolate chips, semisweet chocolate and paraffin in top of double boiler.

Remove candy balls from refrigerator. Hold balls between two forks and dip in melted chocolate. Place on wire cake rack until chocolate coating sets. Store in a cool place, in covered container. Makes 48 balls, or 1¾ pounds.

## DECORATED SUGAR CUBES

*So pretty for a tea table*

| | |
|---|---|
| 1 c. sifted confectioners sugar | Food colors |
| 3 tsp. hot water | Sugar cubes |

Mix confectioners sugar and water; add 1 to 2 drops food color to tint frosting in color desired (red for roses, blue for forget-me-nots, green for leaves—or as you prefer). Mixture should be stiff, colors should be dainty pastels.

With cake decorating tubes, make tiny flower and leaf designs on sugar cubes (see photo in this book).

# CONFECTIONS

# Confections—First Cousins of Candy

No candy cookbook would be complete without the sugared and spiced nuts and all the delicious fruit confections which many mothers substitute for fruit cake. They usually are less work to make. Confections make exquisite party refreshments or great snacks for informal gatherings—it just depends on how you present them.

Treat your guests to Hot Spiced Nuts at the end of a meal or for evening refreshments. While the candied nuts are good cold, the home economist-homemaker who contributed the recipe prefers to serve them warm. "I excuse myself for a few minutes after a meal," she confides. "The aroma that comes from the kitchen while I sugar the nuts is tantalizing," she adds, "and when I return with the warm spicy-fragrant nuts, my guests can scarcely believe I fixed them in the short time I was in the kitchen."

Confection rolls get top billing with the imaginative hostess, too. You can make the rolls ahead, wrap them in waxed paper and put them in the refrigerator where they'll keep for a day or two—then just slice them at serving time while the coffee perks. Another make-ahead is a specialty from the Northwest—fruit confections that are set with gelatin. We predict they'll be favorites of yours as soon as you try them.

We're keen about dainty meringues, especially our bright Cranberry Meringues, which are both luscious and festive-looking. The All-American specialties made with popcorn have a place here, too. One of the best is a caramel popcorn that develops its flavor when heated in a low oven. Cereal confections, so easy to make and inexpensive, also appear in this section, along with sweet treats made with bread, and cookie or cracker crumbs. There are two, Napoleon Cremes and Frozen Chocolate Cups, so chocolatey and rich, you could serve them for dessert for a change with a company dinner.

And, like other recipes in this book, confections make great gifts. Take elegant Glazed Almonds, coated with a shiny caramel glaze—now there's a treat. A box of them would be perfect for that friend who has everything.

# Sugared and Spiced Nuts

There's an old California ranch custom that's just too good ever to go out of style—placing a dish of sugared walnuts on a table in the living room for guests to nibble on. Because sugared or spiced nuts are so popular, new ways of fixing them frequently appear and win local fame.

Many of the nut confections in our collection are cherished recipes from women who live in areas where nut trees grow and yield a bounty of their fruit. But we have some from women who gather their nuts in supermarkets, too. You can make these superior snacks no matter where you live. Your family and friends will like them because they're really good.

## FROSTED PECANS

*Sour cream boosts flavors in these sweet-coated nuts. Try them*

| | |
|---|---|
| ½ c. dairy sour cream | 1½ tsp. vanilla |
| 1½ c. sugar | 3 c. pecan halves |

Combine sour cream, sugar and vanilla in 2-qt. heavy saucepan. Cook to soft ball stage (234°), stirring frequently to prevent scorching.

Add pecans and stir to coat. Turn onto buttered baking sheet and separate with 2 forks. Package and freeze in airtight containers, if you like. Makes about 1¼ pounds.

## Variation

**Frosted Sour Cream Walnuts** Substitute walnut halves for the pecans.

## CINNAMON CANDIED NUTS

*It's cinnamon/sour cream candy coating that makes the nuts so good*

| | |
|---|---|
| 1½ c. sugar | 1 tsp. vanilla |
| ½ c. dairy sour cream | 1 tsp. ground cinnamon |
| 2 tblsp. butter | 1½ c. pecan or walnut halves |
| ¼ tsp. salt | |

Combine sugar, sour cream, butter and salt in 2-qt. heavy saucepan. Place over medium-high heat and stir until sugar is dissolved; then cook to soft ball stage (236°) over medium-low heat. Remove from heat and let stand without stirring for 15 minutes.

Stir in vanilla and cinnamon; continue stirring until mixture begins to thicken and lose its sheen. At this point add the nuts and blend in, making sure they are all covered.

Turn nuts onto 2 lightly buttered baking sheets, making little islands. (With a fork and spoon you can quickly separate these into individual nuts, if you like.) Let stand to harden and dry. Store in covered container, in refrigerator or freezer. Makes 1¼ pounds.

N O T E : Candied nuts are nicer if near-perfect halves of pecans are used; walnut halves or quarters also make nice bite-size nibbles.

## CRISP HONEY NUTS

*Faint honey taste is pleasant; heat to make nuts crisp, full-flavored*

| | |
|---|---|
| 1½ c. sugar | 3 c. walnuts |
| ¼ c. honey | ½ tsp. vanilla |
| ½ c. water | |

Combine sugar, honey and water in 2-qt. heavy saucepan. Bring to a boil, stirring constantly. Then cook to the soft ball stage (238°) without stirring.

Meanwhile, spread nuts in shallow pan and heat in preheated moderate oven (375°) 5 minutes, stirring once.

Remove candy mixture from heat; beat by hand 1 minute, or just until mixture starts to get creamy.

Quickly add vanilla and warm nuts; stir to coat nuts with candy. Turn onto a buttered baking sheet or into a buttered 15½ × 10½ ×1" jelly roll pan; separate with forks into individual pieces. Store in covered container, in refrigerator or freezer. Makes about 30 pieces, or 1½ pounds.

## WALNUT MINTS

*You'll like this peppermint-flavored candy coating for walnuts*

| | |
|---|---|
| 1 c. sugar | 6 large marshmallows |
| ½ c. water | 5 drops oil of peppermint or |
| 1 tblsp. light corn syrup | ½ tsp. peppermint extract |
| ½ tsp. salt | 3 c. walnut halves or pieces |

Combine sugar, water, corn syrup and salt in a 2-qt. heavy saucepan. Place over low to medium heat and stir until sugar is dissolved, then cook to the soft ball stage (234 to 236°).

Remove from heat; add marshmallows and stir until melted. Add flavoring and nuts, stirring only until well combined.

Drop by teaspoonfuls onto waxed paper. If mixture starts to set, return to heat for a minute and add a few drops of boiling water. Store in covered container, in refrigerator or freezer. Makes about 36 patties or 1¼ pounds.

## ORANGE WALNUTS

*Fresh orange juice and peel are the flavor secret of these tasty nuts*

| | |
|---|---|
| 1½ c. sugar | 1 tsp. grated orange peel |
| ½ c. orange juice | ½ tsp. vanilla |
| Few drops yellow food color (optional) | 3 c. walnut halves |

Combine sugar and orange juice in 2-qt. heavy saucepan. Cook to soft ball stage (240°). Add a little food color to tint a delicate orange.

Remove from heat, add orange peel, vanilla and walnut halves. Stir until syrup begins to look cloudy. Before it hardens, spread mixture on a waxed paper lined baking sheet so nuts do not overlap. When cool, break in bite-size pieces. Store in covered container, in refrigerator or freezer. Makes about 1 pound.

## KUMEH (GRAPE WALNUTS)

*Amethyst candy holds walnuts in this unusual fruit-nut confection*

1 c. sugar
½ c. grape juice
2 c. walnut halves

Add sugar to grape juice and cook in 2-qt. heavy saucepan to the firm ball stage (248°).

Remove from heat and pour over walnuts. Stir until syrup becomes creamy and thick. Spread mixture on buttered baking sheet to harden, then break in individual pieces. Store in covered container, in refrigerator or freezer. Makes 26 pieces, or about 1 pound.

## SUGARED NUTS

*Nibblers like these candied nuts because they're so good—hostesses like them because they're so easy to fix*

| | |
|---|---|
| 3 c. walnut halves | 1 c. water |
| 1½ c. pecan halves | ¼ tsp. ground cinnamon |
| 2 c. sugar | |

Mix ingredients in a 12″ heavy skillet. Cook until water disappears and nuts have a sugary appearance. Remove from heat and pour nuts onto a greased baking sheet. Separate quickly with 2 forks. Cool and store in covered container, in refrigerator or freezer. Makes 4½ to 5 cups.

## GLAZED ALMONDS

*Perfect gift for fastidious friends; easier to make than you think*

| | |
|---|---|
| 2 c. whole almonds | 1 tsp. salt |
| 2 c. sugar | 1 tsp. ground nutmeg (optional) |

Spread almonds in a 15½ × 10½ × 1″ jelly roll pan and place in preheated moderate oven (350°) 10 to 12 minutes. Turn out into another lightly buttered jelly roll pan and hold in a warm place.

Meanwhile, place sugar in a 10″ heavy skillet, or 3-qt. heavy saucepan, over medium-high heat. Stir constantly with a wooden spoon until sugar changes to a golden amber liquid, about 10 minutes.

Remove from heat; quickly stir in salt and nutmeg, then pour over toasted almonds, being careful to coat every nut with the glaze. Let stand until cold, then invert pan (press against bottom and the sheet of glazed almonds will fall out). Break in pieces; store between layers of waxed paper in tightly covered container. Makes about 1¼ pounds.

## HOT SPICED NUTS

*They're wonderful warm or cold*

1 c. sugar
1 tsp. ground cinnamon
6 tblsp. milk
½ tsp. vanilla

3 c. dry roasted mixed unsalted
  nuts (walnuts, pecans,
  almonds, cashews, etc.)

Combine sugar, cinnamon and milk in 2-qt. heavy saucepan. Bring to a boil, stirring constantly. Continue cooking at a fairly low boil to the soft ball stage (236°).

Remove from heat; add vanilla and nuts and stir until creamy. Turn out on waxed paper or lightly buttered baking sheet and separate. Serve warm or cold. Store in covered container, in refrigerator or freezer. Makes 1¼ pounds.

## SPICY MIXED NUTS

*Salted mixed nuts—all sugared and spiced—are nice!*

1 c. sugar
½ tsp. ground cinnamon
¼ c. evaporated milk

2 tsp. water
1½ c. salted mixed nuts
½ tsp. vanilla

Combine sugar, cinnamon, evaporated milk and water in a 2-qt. heavy saucepan. Place over medium or medium-low heat and cook to the soft ball stage (236 to 238°), stirring constantly to prevent curdling.

Remove from heat; mix in nuts and vanilla. Let stand 15 minutes, then stir with a wooden spoon until mixture thickens. Pour at once onto waxed paper-lined baking sheet, spreading as thinly as possible. When cool, break in bite-size pieces. Store in covered container, in refrigerator or freezer. Makes 1 pound.

NOTE: If mixed nuts contain Brazil nuts, cut them in 2 or 3 pieces.

## Variation

**Spicy Peanuts** Instead of the salted mixed nuts, use red-skinned salted Spanish peanuts.

## DIFFERENT CANDIED NUTS

*Let the children fix this snack*

1 (6 oz.) pkg. chocolate chips
1 (6 oz.) pkg. butterscotch-
flavored morsels

1 tblsp. smooth or crunchy
peanut butter
1½ c. salted mixed nuts

Combine all ingredients, except nuts, in top of double boiler. Heat, stirring occasionally until bits are melted and blended with peanut butter.

Add nuts all at once and stir until thoroughly coated.

Drop by teaspoonfuls onto waxed paper-lined baking sheet. Store in covered container, in refrigerator or freezer. Makes 42 pieces, or about 1¼ pounds.

N O T E : If mixed nuts contain Brazil nuts, cut them in 2 or 3 pieces.


## SUGARED PEANUTS

*Sugary peanuts with glint of gold please youngsters who like snacks*

1½ c. sugar
1 c. water

1 c. raw Spanish peanuts,
crushed slightly

Combine 1 c. sugar and ½ c. water in 1½-qt. heavy saucepan. Bring to a boil, stirring constantly. If sugar crystals form on sides of pan, wipe them off. Add peanuts; cook and stir over low heat until syrup becomes grainy.

Remove from heat and pour into coarse sieve, reserving the loose sugar. Keep peanuts warm in oven that has been heated to 250° then turned off.

Place sugar removed in sieving with remaining ½ c. sugar and ½ c. water back into saucepan. Cook to the firm ball stage (245°).

Add peanuts to hot syrup and stir until syrup grains. Pour onto unbuttered baking sheet or marble slab and separate. When cool, store in covered container, in refrigerator or freezer. Makes about 1 pound.

N O T E : When syrup reaches the firm ball stage, you can color and flavor it, if you like, with 3 drops yellow food color and ½ tsp. vanilla.

## CHOCOLATE PEANUTS

*Cocoa-sugar coating makes peanuts special—they're a men's favorite*

3 c. sugar
1 c. milk
¼ c. cocoa, or 1 square
   unsweetened chocolate

1 to 1⅓ c. salted Spanish
   peanuts
1 tsp. vanilla

Melt 1 c. sugar in a 10″ heavy skillet over medium-high heat, stirring constantly until it liquefies and is light brown or amber in color.

Remove from heat just long enough to add ½ c. milk, a few drops at a time at first, stirring vigorously as mixture bubbles up.

Return to heat and add remaining 2 c. sugar, sifted with cocoa, and ½ c. milk. Cook to the soft ball stage (about 238°). Remove from heat; mix in peanuts and vanilla. Let stand 15 minutes to cool slightly, then stir until mixture begins to thicken.

Pour at once into a buttered 13×9×2″ pan, spreading as thinly as possible so that peanuts stand out. Store in covered container, in refrigerator or freezer. Makes about 72 pieces, or 2 pounds.

# Fruit Confections

Fruit confections are not new, but our recipes for them are—or they are revised versions of revered old timers. Dried apricot and apple confections, set with gelatin, rate as great regional favorites on the West Coast. Visitors to the area often ship or carry boxes of them home for gifts to family and friends. But you don't have to live in the far Western states to get these confections. You can make them with the recipes in this section, and many other fruit specials, too! Do try them soon.

## NORTHWESTERN APRICOT CANDY

*If you like apricots you'll enjoy this famous Northwestern treat*

2 (5½ oz.) pkgs. dried apricots (2 c.)
1 c. warm water
2 c. sugar
1 tblsp. cornstarch
⅛ tsp. salt

2 tblsp. unflavored gelatin
½ c. cold water
½ to ⅔ c. chopped or slivered almonds, or chopped walnuts
⅓ c. confectioners sugar (for rolling)

Remove any stems or blemishes from apricots. Soak in warm water 1 hour, then cook slowly in same water until very tender, stirring to avoid scorching. Put through a food mill or sieve. Cook apricot pulp until thick in a 2-qt. heavy saucepan, stirring frequently to avoid scorching.

Mix sugar, cornstarch and salt and add to apricot pulp. Cook until very thick, stirring constantly.

Add gelatin, which has been softened in cold water. Stir until gelatin is dissolved and cook until mixture is again thick. Remove from heat.

Mix in almonds. Turn into a 9×7" shallow glass dish that has been rinsed with cold water. Let stand 24 hours.

Cut candy in rectangular pieces (about 60) and roll in confectioners sugar. Let stand on rack until outside has dried (texture should be slightly chewy). Store in covered container. Makes about 1 pound, 12 ounces, depending on amount of nuts used.

## NORTHWESTERN APPLE CANDY

*Be sure to dry these confections before storing*

| | |
|---|---|
| 4 to 5 unpeeled apples | ⅔ c. coarsely chopped walnuts |
| 2 tblsp. unflavored gelatin | 1 tsp. grated lemon peel |
| ½ c. cold water | 1 tblsp. lemon juice |
| 2 c. sugar | ⅓ c. confectioners sugar (for |
| 1 tblsp. cornstarch | rolling) |
| ⅛ tsp. salt | |

Wash apples; without peeling or coring, cut in small pieces. Cook until very tender in just enough water to avoid scorching. Put through food mill or sieve and measure 2 c. pulp into a 2-qt. heavy saucepan. Cook until thick, stirring often.

Soften gelatin in cold water.

Mix sugar, cornstarch and salt; add to apple pulp. Cook again over low heat, stirring constantly, until mixture is very thick. Add gelatin; stir until gelatin is dissolved and mixture is again thick. Remove from heat.

Stir in walnuts, lemon peel and juice. Turn into an 8″ square shallow glass dish that has been rinsed with cold water. Let stand 24 hours.

Cut in rectangles (about 60). Roll in confectioners sugar, and place on rack until outside is dry. Store in covered container. Makes about 1 pound, 12 ounces.

N O T E : You can use 2 c. sweetened canned applesauce to make this confection, but reduce the amount of sugar from 2 to 1⅓ cups.

## Nuggets of Fruit Gold

You can depend on your guests to ask for the recipe when you serve them Apricot-Orange Balls. The confection carries a sugar-sweet taste accented with a fruity tang.

The Kansas woman who contributed the recipe says she sometimes flattens the golden balls and shapes them like dried apricot halves. But the shape really is not important. This confection deserves your best adjectives—superb, superlative, exceptional, really good. An Oklahoma FARM JOURNAL reader rolls these balls in colored sugar for holiday parties. Green sugar is especially attractive.

## APRICOT-ORANGE BALLS

*With the demand for dried apricots so great, the price tag on them is higher, but they are worth the cost, especially for gala occasions*

| | |
|---|---|
| 1 large orange | 2 c. sugar |
| 3 (5½ oz.) pkgs. dried apricots | ⅔ c. (about) sugar (for rolling) |

Peel orange; remove white lining from peel and membrane from sections; remove any seeds.

Put apricots, orange sections and peel through food chopper using fine or medium blade (alternate ingredients to make grinding easier). Turn into a 3-qt. heavy saucepan; add 2 c. sugar and cook over medium heat about 8 minutes, stirring continuously. At this stage the mixture will drop from spoon in large pieces.

Remove from heat at once and allow to cool 30 minutes, or until a spoonful dropped in sugar can be handled easily and rolled into a ball.

Place ⅔ c. sugar in a small bowl or cup. Using 2 teaspoons, dip a small amount of apricot mixture in sugar with one, pushing it out with the second spoon. Form quickly into a ball. Repeat with remaining apricot mixture. Place on sugar-sprinkled waxed paper to cool and set. Let stand several hours before packing in airtight containers. Makes 7 to 8 dozen balls the diameter of a 50-cent piece, or about 2 pounds.

## APRICOT NUGGETS

*These easy-to-make candies add a tasty note to a plate of confections*

| | |
|---|---|
| 1 lb. confectioners sugar | ½ tsp. vanilla |
| 6 tblsp. melted butter or margarine | 1 (11 oz.) pkg. dried apricots, ground (about 1½ c.) |
| 2 tblsp. orange juice | 1 c. chopped pecans |

Combine sugar, butter, orange juice and vanilla. Add apricots. Mix, then knead in bowl until ingredients are well mixed.

Form into 1″ balls. Roll in chopped nuts. Store in refrigerator or freezer in covered container. Flavor improves with storage. Makes 6 dozen candies.

NOTE: If you like, you can omit the pecans and roll the candy balls in 1½ c. shredded coconut.

## BUTTERED STUFFED DATES

*You'll be surprised how heating dates in butter steps up flavor*

1 (12 oz.) pkg. pitted dates
2 tblsp. butter
⅓ c. (about) salted cashew or
  mixed salted nuts

⅓ c. (about) sifted
  confectioners sugar

Remove any stem ends from dates; set aside.

Melt butter in 8″ heavy skillet over medium heat. Add dates, one at a time, and cook 6 to 8 minutes, stirring with a rubber spatula. Remove from heat and let stand in skillet to cool until easy to handle.

Meanwhile, sort out 42 perfect cashews, peanuts or almonds. Stuff each date with 1 nut (you may need more for large dates).

Drop stuffed dates, about 6 at a time, into confectioners sugar; shake off any excess sugar. Continue until all dates are coated. Wrap individually in waxed paper, twisting ends. Makes about 42 pieces, depending on number of dates in package, or 1 pound.

NOTE: You may also stuff dates with small or halved Brazil nuts, but be sure to heat them first with butter and a little salt.

## WALNUT-STUFFED PRUNES

*Sugar coating melts during the time the stuffed fruit mellows*

1 lb. dried prunes
1 c. walnut pieces

18 marshmallows, cut in pieces
¼ c. sugar

Slit sides of soft dried prunes and carefully remove pits. Stuff with walnut and marshmallow pieces. Roll in sugar.

Place in waxed paper-lined coffee cans or other containers. Cover tightly and store in a cool place several days or weeks. Makes about 48, depending on size of prunes.

NOTE: To cut up marshmallows easily, dip scissors in cold water.

## CHOCOLATE RAISIN CLUSTERS

*Chocolate holds raisins in irresistible clusters—easy to fix*

| | |
|---|---|
| 1 (6 oz.) pkg. chocolate chips | 2 tblsp. confectioners sugar |
| ¼ c. light corn syrup | 2 c. seedless raisins |
| 1½ tsp. vanilla | |

Combine chocolate chips and syrup in top of double boiler over hot water. Set over low heat. Stir until chocolate is melted. Remove from heat.

Add vanilla, confectioners sugar and raisins. Stir to coat with chocolate.

Drop from teaspoon onto buttered baking sheet. Chill. Store in a cool place, in a covered container. Makes 30 pieces, about 1¼ pounds.

## SLICE 'N SERVE DATE ROLLS

*Candied cherries add bright color to this luscious date-nut roll*

| | |
|---|---|
| ½ lb. white confection coating (see Index) | 1 c. halved dates |
| | 1 c. candied cherries |
| 2 tblsp. milk | ½ c. finely chopped pecans |

Combine coating with milk in top of double boiler; melt over boiling water. Stir until smooth. Remove from heat and stir in dates and cherries.

Divide mixture equally on 2 sheets of waxed paper. Shape each part into a 10" log, using waxed paper to help shape logs.

Coat each with ¼ c. pecans. Chill until set. To serve, cut in ¼ to ½" slices. Makes 2 logs, or about 50 pieces.

## FRUIT CONFECTION ROLL

*Dried fruits never tasted better than they do in this appetizing roll*

| | |
|---|---|
| ½ lb. white confection coating (see Index) | ½ c. raisins |
| | ½ c. broken nuts |
| 2 tblsp. milk | ½ c. flaked coconut |
| 1 c. ground dried apricots | |

Combine coating and milk; melt in top of double boiler over boiling water. Stir until smooth. Remove from lower part of double boiler and stir in fruit and broken nuts.

Divide mixture in half; place on 2 sheets of waxed paper. Shape each half in a 10″ roll, using waxed paper to help in the shaping.

Coat each with ¼ c. coconut. Chill until set. To serve, cut in ½″ slices. Makes 2 logs, or about 40 pieces.

## HONEYED FRUIT LOG

*Graham cracker crumbs and honey join dried fruits in this treat*

½ c. ground dates
1 c. ground dried apricots
½ c. dried currants

½ c. graham cracker crumbs
½ c. honey
½ c. flaked coconut

Combine all ingredients, except coconut. Blend thoroughly.

Place on waxed paper and shape in a 16″ roll, using waxed paper to help in the shaping.

Coat with coconut. Wrap with waxed paper and chill several hours. To serve, cut in ½″ slices. Makes 1 (16″) log, or about 32 pieces.

## *Variation*

**Honeyed Fruit Balls** Shape mixture in small balls instead of a log; roll in coconut. Makes about 30 balls.

## APRICOT LOGS

*Put the golden rolls in the freezer to firm up before slicing*

2 (5½ oz.) pkgs. dried apricots
1 lb. confectioners sugar
6 tblsp. melted butter
2 tblsp. frozen orange juice
   concentrate

1 tsp. vanilla
1 c. chopped pecans

Remove any stems or blemishes from apricots; put apricots through food chopper using fine blade.

Combine apricots, sugar, butter, orange juice concentrate and vanilla in a 3-qt. bowl. Mix, then knead in bowl until ingredients are well blended (1 or 2 tsp. more orange juice concentrate may be added if necessary to make a dough-like consistency).

Spread nuts evenly on 4 pieces of waxed paper, each about 12″ long. Divide apricot mixture in 4 parts. Roll one part between lightly buttered palms, making a roll about 6″ long. Place on nut-covered paper; continue to roll, working from center to ends while rolling and pressing into the nuts to make a log about 10" long. Lift log onto 12" strip of aluminum foil and wrap, twisting ends. Let set in freezer. Repeat with remaining portions of mixture.

Cut logs in bite-size pieces and store either in refrigerator or freezer. Makes about 6 dozen pieces, or 2 pounds.

## FRUIT/NUT ROLLS

*Apricots provide a tang that makes this date/nut roll extra good*

| | |
|---|---|
| 1 lb. seeded dates, cut in small pieces | 2 c. sugar |
| | 1 c. milk |
| 6 dried apricot halves, cut in small pieces | ¼ tsp. salt |
| | 2 tsp. vanilla |
| 1 lb. walnuts, chopped or ground (3 c.) | |

Prepare dried fruits and nuts and set aside.

Combine sugar, milk and salt in a 2-qt. heavy saucepan; cook to soft ball stage (236°). Add dates and stir well.

Remove from heat and add 2 c. nuts, apricots and vanilla. Stir until thoroughly mixed; set aside to cool.

Line 3 (12") strips of aluminum foil with similar size strips of waxed paper. Sprinkle ⅓ c. nuts on each.

When fruit confection has cooled enough to handle, divide in thirds. Lightly butter palms of hands; work one portion of mixture into a ball, then into a roll about 6" long; place on nut-covered paper. Holding paper with one hand, continue rolling with flat palm and fingers of other hand, working from middle to outside of roll, until it's about 1" in diameter, pressing nuts into surface for bark effect. Wrap tightly in paper and foil. Repeat with other two portions of mixture.

Chill thoroughly in freezer or refrigerator before cutting in ½" pieces. Makes about 6 dozen pieces, or 3 pounds.

## Variation

**Chocolate Dipped Fruit/Nut Confection** You can work the entire amount of nuts into the mixture and shape into rolls as directed. Chill them for several hours, then cut in ¾" slices and dip them in melted sweet chocolate (see Dipping Chocolates in Index).

# Heirloom Fruit Confections

A FARM JOURNAL friend from California shares her heirloom recipes for Apricot/Almond Favorites and Fruit/Nut Sausage Candy. They came originally from an elderly neighbor who emigrated from Poland to the United States. Once you taste the confections you'll agree the recipes were worth bringing along from a faraway home.

The keeping qualities of these and other confections made with dried fruits are excellent when you put them in airtight containers and store in the freezer or refrigerator. Exposure to air, when you arrange them on a plate or tray for serving, sometimes makes them too moist to eat neatly from the hand. There is a quick and sure remedy. Just roll the pieces in confectioners sugar to coat thoroughly.

## APRICOT/ALMOND FAVORITES

*Apricot/orange-flavored gold with the crunch of ground almonds*

| | |
|---|---|
| 1 c. dried apricots | ¼ c. ground candied orange |
| ⅔ c. warm water | peel |
| ½ c. ground almonds | 1¼ c. sugar |

Remove any stems or blemishes from apricots. Cut with scissors into 4 strips each. Add warm water and let stand several hours, or overnight (water should be mostly absorbed).

Put apricots, almonds and orange peel through food chopper, using fine or medium blade (this helps to mix them thoroughly).

Place ground mixture and 1 c. sugar in 2-qt. heavy saucepan. Stir over medium-low heat, cooking until thick, 10 to 12 minutes. As it thickens, mixture should be stirred constantly to avoid scorching. Let cool until it can be handled easily.

Sprinkle a piece of waxed paper with remaining ¼ c. sugar. Take out half of apricot mixture and roll in buttered palms of hands, making a 6″ roll; place on sugared paper. Holding paper with one hand, continue to roll, exerting pressure from middle to each end, until the roll is about 1″ in diameter and is coated with sugar.

Roll up in aluminum foil and place in freezer or refrigerator to firm and ripen. Repeat procedure with remaining half of candy,

adding more sugar if necessary. When ready to serve, slice in ½"
pieces. Makes about 32 pieces, or 1 pound.

## FRUIT/NUT SAUSAGE CANDY

*They'll like this sweet "sausage" fixed with fruits and nuts*

| | |
|---|---|
| 1 lb. seeded prunes | ½ c. raisins |
| ¾ c. blanched almonds | ¾ c. candied lemon peel |
| ⅓ c. candied orange peel | ½ c. (about) confectioners or |
| ½ c. dried light figs |     granulated sugar (for coating) |

Put all ingredients, except sugar, through food chopper, using fine
blade; alternate ingredients (nuts and peels help to force softer
fruits through). Turn into 3-qt. bowl and mix or knead until
thoroughly blended.

Place 2 (12") lengths of waxed paper on 2 (12") lengths of
aluminum foil. Sprinkle with ¼ c. sugar (use sieve or sugar
shaker). Pick up half of candy mixture in buttered palms of hands;
form it into a ball, then into a roll 5 to 6" long. Place on sugared
paper; hold paper firm with one hand, and roll with other hand
(using palm and fingers out straight) working from middle to ends
of roll until it is 1 to 1¼" in diameter. Slip waxed paper from
under roll, and use aluminum foil to make a firm wrap. (If roll
is limp, put on tray and slip into freezer.) Repeat with remaining
half of mixture. Let ripen several days in refrigerator. To serve,
cut in ½" slices. Makes about 50 pieces, or 2¼ pounds.

N O T E : If candy is too moist after being exposed to air, roll
in confectioners sugar.

## Variation

**Gingered Prune Sausage Candy**   Add 2 tblsp. ground preserved gin-
ger to Fruit/Nut Sausage Candy.

## BOLOGNA CANDY

*It looks like a good summer sausage but it's an elegant, rich candy*

| | |
|---|---|
| 2 c. sugar | 1 c. flaked coconut |
| 1 c. milk | ½ c. chopped nuts |
| 1 lb. dates (2½ c.) | |

Combine sugar and milk in 2-qt. heavy saucepan. Cook over
medium heat to soft ball stage (234°), stirring occasionally.

Add dates and cook, stirring constantly, until mixture is very thick and leaves the side of pan when stirred.

Remove from heat. Stir in coconut and nuts. Cool slightly. Turn out on wet towel. When cool enough to handle and hold shape, roll up in towel. Place in refrigerator and chill.

Make a roll 2" in diameter and about 18" long like rolls of cookie dough. Cut in slices to serve. Makes 2¼ pounds.

## PIONEER FRUIT BARS

*The orange in this confection points up luscious fruit flavors*

| | |
|---|---|
| 1 lb. raisins | 1 orange, juice and peel |
| ½ lb. figs | 1 c. broken walnuts |
| ½ lb. pitted dates | Confectioners sugar (for rolling) |
| 1 c. seeded prunes | |

Put raisins, figs, dates, prunes and orange peel through food mill, using fine blade. Blend thoroughly with orange juice and walnuts.

Press into 2 buttered 9" square pans. Cut contents of each pan in bars about 3×1"; let stand in a cool place at least 24 hours to blend and mellow flavors. To serve, roll bars in confectioners sugar. Makes 56 bars, or about 3 pounds.

NOTE: You can shape Pioneer Fruit Bar mixture in balls, if you like (makes about 100 balls). And you can coat either the bars or balls with melted chocolate (see Index for Dipping Chocolates).

## CARAMEL APPLES ON STICKS

*A simple, inexpensive way to make candy-coated apples. They're at their best eaten the day you make them*

| | |
|---|---|
| 15 to 20 small red apples | 1 c. light corn syrup |
| 4 c. sugar | 2⅔ c. evaporated milk |

Select small apples free from blemishes; wash and dry thoroughly; do not peel. Insert wooden skewers in stem ends.

Combine sugar, corn syrup and ⅔ c. evaporated milk in a 3-qt. heavy saucepan; stir to blend well. Heat slowly until sugar dissolves, stirring constantly. Then cook briskly to a thick syrup, stirring constantly.

Add remaining 2 c. evaporated milk slowly (keep mixture boiling briskly) and cook to the firm ball stage (242°). Stir constantly to prevent scorching.

Remove from heat; let stand until candy stops bubbling. Working quickly, dip apples, one at a time, in caramel syrup. Twist to remove any surplus and to make a smooth coating. Place on buttered heavy-duty aluminum foil or buttered baking sheets. (If caramel coating becomes too hard for dipping, add a little evaporated milk and reheat, stirring to keep smooth. The caramel should be kept quite hot so coating will not be too heavy.) Makes 15 to 20 caramel apples.

## CRANBERRY MERINGUES

*Serve these delicious beauties at your Christmas open house*

    1 c. cranberries (50 to 60)
    1 egg white
    1 c. sifted confectioners sugar

Select rosy-red cranberries of similar size; wash, remove any stems and dry thoroughly.

Put egg white and confectioners sugar in mixing bowl; stir to combine. Then beat until very stiff, about 5 minutes with an electric beater at medium speed. Meringue should be stiff enough so that it will hold a swirl when a cranberry is dipped into it and dropped from the point of a spoon.

Rinse a baking sheet with warm water, leaving surface damp; cover with plain brown paper; or use a non-stick pan.

Drop cranberries one at a time into meringue and roll with a teaspoon until coated; dip out with same spoon and drop onto baking sheet, making a swirl over the top. Drop no more than 18 or 20 meringues at a time (you will have three bakings).

Bake in preheated very slow oven (250°) 8 to 10 minutes, or until meringues have a dry appearance (do not try to brown them). You can store the meringues in refrigerator or freeze them for up to 1 month. Remove from container or wrapping before defrosting. Makes 50 to 60 meringues.

NOTE: Meringue mixture may be tinted pink with 1 or 2 drops red food color. Serve in individual tiny (bonbon) paper cups for a festive occasion.

*Variation*

**Ripe Gooseberry Meringues** Substitute large ripe or nearly ripe gooseberries for the cranberries, being careful to remove all stems and blossom ends. You can tint the meringue mixture with a few drops of green food color, if you like.

## How to Candy Grapefruit Peel

Select and wash thick-skinned grapefruit. Cut into quarters and remove pulp. Put peel in saucepan; cover with cold water. Weight down peel with a plate. Let stand several hours or overnight. Drain.

With scissors, cut peel into strips about ¼" wide.

Cover peel with cold water and slowly bring to a simmer (180°) in a saucepan. Remove from heat, cover pan and let stand about 1 hour; drain. Repeat process until peel no longer tastes bitter (about 3 times).

Cover again with water and boil until yellow peel is tender, about 15 minutes. Drain well in colander. Press out water. Pack peel firmly into measuring cup to measure.

Return peel to saucepan. For each cup of peel, add 1 cup of sugar. Place over medium heat; stir until sugar has dissolved (peel forms its own liquid).

Cook peel over medium heat, stirring frequently, until sugar syrup is concentrated; reduce heat to low (syrup should boil gently). Continue cooking until the grapefruit peel is semitransparent and most of the sugar syrup has boiled away.

Drain in colander. Separate pieces of peel on baking sheets and allow to stand until pieces feel fairly dry. Sprinkle with enough sugar to give a crystalline look.

Store in tightly covered cans, or in plastic bags in the freezer.

## CANDIED ORANGE PEEL

*For an elegant bridge snack dip candied peel in melted chocolate*

| | |
|---|---|
| 6 medium oranges | 2½ c. sugar |
| 1 tblsp. salt | ½ c. water |
| 4 c. water | |

Cut each orange lengthwise in half; then cut each half in thirds.

Remove pulp with a spoon (save it to use in a fruit cup or to combine with flaked coconut for dessert). Remove much of the white membrane from peel with knife to reduce bitter taste.

Add salt to 4 c. water; add peel. Weight down with plate, topped with glass fruit jar filled with water to keep peel immersed. Let stand overnight.

Next day, drain and wash thoroughly in cold water. Cover with cold water and heat to a boil. Drain. Repeat this procedure three times (this reduces bitter taste).

Cut peel in strips with kitchen scissors. You will have about 2 c. peel. Combine with 2 c. sugar and ½ c. water. Heat, stirring constantly until sugar dissolves. Then cook slowly until peel is translucent and absorbs most of the syrup. (Watch carefully to avoid burning.)

Drain; roll strips in remaining ½ c. sugar. Dry thoroughly on wire rack. Store in covered container. Makes about 2½ cups.

## NO-COOK FRUIT BALLS

*Apricot and prune flavors complement each other in this easy treat*

| | |
|---|---|
| ½ c. diced dried apricots | 2 tsp. grated orange peel |
| ½ c. diced prunes | 2¾ c. confectioners sugar |
| ½ c. sweetened condensed milk | 1 c. shredded coconut |
| 2 tsp. frozen orange juice concentrate | |

Put apricots and prunes through food chopper; you should have 1 c. firmly packed.

Combine condensed milk (not evaporated), orange juice concentrate and peel in a 2-qt. bowl. Add sugar gradually; add dried fruits and mix well. Form into a soft ball. Drop from a teaspoon into small bowl filled with coconut; roll into small balls ¾ to 1" in diameter.

Place in freezer or refrigerator to set and hold shape. Makes about 3½ dozen balls, or 1½ pounds.

# Popcorn Confections

American Indians introduced our early colonists to corn that popped over heat. From that faraway beginning many wonderful popcorn snacks developed—among them, the sweet popcorn confections. Crackerjack is one that pleases young people from one generation to the next. Try our version, Honeyed Popcorn; also Holiday Popcorn Crunch, which combines popped corn with nuts for an unforgettable snack. And if you're working in the kitchen, run a pan of caramel corn in the oven to bake slowly. It's a best-ever confection.

## HOLIDAY POPCORN CRUNCH

*They'll not stop eating until it's all gone—it's simply irresistible*

⅔ c. sugar
½ c. butter or margarine
  (1 stick)
¼ c. light corn syrup

½ tsp. vanilla
⅔ c. pecans
⅓ c. almonds
4 c. popped corn

Combine sugar, margarine and corn syrup in 1½-qt. heavy saucepan. Bring to a boil over medium heat, stirring constantly until sugar dissolves and mixture comes to a boil. Continue cooking, stirring occasionally, to the soft crack stage (290°). Mixture will have a light caramel color.

Remove from heat and stir in vanilla.

Meanwhile, toast nuts in slow oven (300°) until almonds are light brown. Spread popped corn and nuts on lightly greased baking sheet.

Pour hot syrup over popped corn and nuts. With two tablespoons, toss corn and nuts to completely coat with syrup. Let cool.

Break popped corn and nuts apart and store, as soon as cool, in a tightly covered container. Makes about 5 cups, or 1 pound.

## HONEYED POPCORN

*Honey makes these different. Serve to children who come to visit*

| | |
|---|---|
| 3 qts. popped corn | 1 tsp. salt |
| 1½ c. sugar | 2 tblsp. butter or margarine |
| ½ c. honey | 1 tsp. vanilla |

Turn popped corn into bowl.

Combine sugar, honey and salt in small saucepan. Heat and stir to dissolve sugar. Boil to hard ball stage (260°). Add butter and vanilla. Pour syrup over popped corn, stirring gently to coat kernels.

Drop by tablespoonfuls onto waxed paper. When popcorn is cool enough to handle, butter hands and quickly shape into bite-size balls. Store in airtight container at room temperature. Makes 24 balls.

## OVEN-MADE CARAMEL CORN

*Be ready for evening callers—make this inexpensive snack the new, easy way. A fine gift to mail to youngsters away at school*

| | |
|---|---|
| 5 qts. popped corn | ½ c. light corn syrup |
| 1 c. butter or margarine | 1 tsp. salt |
| (2 sticks) | ½ tsp. baking soda |
| 2 c. brown sugar, firmly packed | |

Spread freshly popped corn in a large, shallow sheet pan. Put in a very slow oven (250°) to keep warm and crisp.

Combine butter, brown sugar, corn syrup and salt in 2-qt. heavy saucepan. Place on medium heat, stirring until sugar dissolves. Continue to boil to the firm ball stage (248°), about 5 minutes.

Remove from heat and stir in baking soda. Syrup will foam.

Take popped corn from oven and pour hot caramel mixture over it in a fine stream. Stir to mix well. Return to oven for 45 to 50 minutes, stirring every 15 minutes. Cool and serve, or store.

To store, pour into airtight containers and set in a cold place. Makes about 5 quarts, or almost 2 pounds.

## CARAMEL POPCORN

*An inexpensive snack for everyone—freezes well in airtight cans*

| | |
|---|---|
| 1½ c. white sugar | ¼ c. butter or margarine |
| 1 c. brown sugar, firmly packed | (½ stick) |
| ⅔ c. dark corn syrup | 1 tsp. baking soda |
| ¾ c. water | 1 tsp. vanilla |
| 1 tsp. salt | 7 qts. popped corn |

Combine white and brown sugars, corn syrup and water in 2-qt. heavy saucepan. Cook over medium heat, stirring frequently and wiping sides of pan with damp pastry brush, until mixture reaches soft crack stage (290°).

Stir in salt (1 tsp. is correct) and continue cooking at a steady, low boil to the hard crack stage (300°).

Remove from heat and stir in butter, baking soda and vanilla until well blended. Slowly pour over popped corn, stirring until kernels are well coated.

Turn onto a clean, cool surface and spread out. When cold, break in pieces. Makes about 7 quarts caramel corn.

## HONEYED POPCORN BALLS

*Also try our Pop-Nut Jumbles for a snackers' dream-come-true treat*

| | |
|---|---|
| 1½ qts. unbuttered popped corn, salted | ¼ c. honey or light or dark corn syrup |
| ½ c. brown sugar | ⅓ c. water |
| ½ c. white sugar | 1 tblsp. butter |

Put popped corn in a large bowl or metal dishpan; place in warm oven (225°).

Combine sugars, honey and water in 2-qt. heavy saucepan. Heat slowly, stirring until sugar is dissolved. Cook to firm ball stage (242°). Add butter and stir only enough to mix. Slowly pour the hot syrup over warm popped corn; mix thoroughly.

With buttered palms and fingers, shape immediately into balls slightly larger than a baseball, using as little pressure as possible. Makes 12 popcorn balls.

## Variation

**Pop-Nut Jumble**  Use the same amount of popped corn, but omit the salt. Add 1½ c. mixed salted nuts. Hold in warm oven (225°) while preparing syrup as for Honeyed Popcorn Balls. Add syrup and mix in thoroughly but leave mixture in chunky pieces (bite-size and larger). Turn out onto a large board covered with foil. Let cool, then break apart in large pieces; store in airtight tin cans (coffee cans are good). Makes about 2 quarts.

## FARMHOUSE POPCORN BALLS

*Balls have that good old-fashioned flavor—the kind Grandma made*

| | |
|---|---|
| 2 c. sugar | ½ c. butter or margarine |
| ⅔ c. water | (1 stick) |
| 1½ tsp. salt | ½ tsp. vanilla |
| ⅔ c. light corn syrup or honey | 4 qts. warm popped corn |

Combine sugar, water, salt, corn syrup and butter in 2-qt. heavy saucepan. Bring to a boil, stirring until sugar is dissolved. Continue cooking without stirring at a low boil until mixture reaches the hard ball stage (268°). Add vanilla.

Pour hot candy mixture over freshly popped corn kept warm in a slow (200°) oven; mix well. Wet hands and shape into balls, about 2½" in diameter. Makes 30.

## SUGAR COATED POPCORN

*Make this snack when neighbors call and say they're coming over*

| | |
|---|---|
| 2 tblsp. butter | ⅓ c. water |
| 1½ c. brown sugar | 4 qts. popped corn |
| ½ tsp. salt | |

Melt butter in 2-qt. heavy saucepan; add sugar, salt and water and bring to a boil. Boil 16 minutes, or until mixture reaches the soft ball stage (240°).

Pour over popped corn and stir until every kernel is coated with sugary mixture. Cool 5 to 10 minutes, or until sugar coating dries. Makes about 4 quarts.

## POPCORN NIBBLE-ONS

*This makes a fine candy go-with—complements the sweet taste*

| | |
|---|---|
| 3 qts. popped corn | ½ tsp. bottled steak sauce |
| 2 c. cheese snack crackers or nibblers | ½ tsp. garlic salt |
| | ½ tsp. onion salt |
| 2 c. salted Spanish peanuts | ½ tsp. curry powder |
| 2 c. pretzel sticks | ½ tsp. salt |
| ⅓ c. melted butter | |

Combine popped corn, crackers, peanuts and pretzel sticks in large roasting pan.

Combine remaining ingredients and add to first mixture. Toss to mix.

Heat in very slow oven (250°) about 1 hour, stirring every 15 minutes. Cool. Store in airtight container. Makes about 4½ quarts.

NOTE: These Popcorn Nibble-Ons can be made ahead, packed in airtight containers and stored in the freezer. They will keep for several months, and are good to have on hand to serve guests.

## POPCORN-ON-STICKS

*Perfect for party favors. Children and adults like to munch on them*

| | |
|---|---|
| 1½ c. sugar | ¼ tsp. salt |
| ¾ c. light corn syrup | 3 tblsp. butter |
| ½ c. water | 2½ qts. popped corn |

Combine sugar, corn syrup, water and salt in 2-qt. heavy saucepan. Place over low heat, stirring until mixture boils. Cook without stirring to the soft crack stage (270°).

Remove from heat; add butter, stirring only enough to combine with syrup.

Pour syrup over popped corn in a large greased bowl, using a wooden spoon to mix until every kernel is coated. For attractive results, divide syrup in 3 parts; delicately tint each with a few drops of food color, such as green, red and yellow.

With lightly greased hands, form popcorn cylinders to put on sticks; don't press too hard. Or press the syrup-coated corn into small greased juice cans; remove can bottoms to push out cylinders.

Insert a wooden skewer into every cylinder of popped corn. Makes about 6.

## FRUIT/NUT POPCORN SQUARES

*Here's a colorful, crisp confection that looks like Christmas*

| | |
|---|---|
| 1½ c. sugar | 1 tsp. vanilla |
| ½ c. light or dark corn syrup | 6 c. popped corn |
| ½ c. water | 1 c. mixed nuts |
| 2 tblsp. butter or margarine | 2 c. mixed candied fruit |

Combine sugar, corn syrup and water in 2-qt. heavy saucepan; stir until sugar is dissolved. Cook to the soft crack stage (270°).

Remove from heat; add butter and vanilla. Pour over warm freshly popped corn, nuts and fruit, stirring to coat evenly with syrup.

Press into buttered 13×9×2″ pan; cut in 1½″ squares while still warm. Makes about 40 pieces, or 2 pounds.

## POPCORN NUT BRITTLE

*Break into chunks or bite-size pieces*

| | |
|---|---|
| 1½ c. sugar | 1 c. toasted slivered almonds |
| ½ c. light corn syrup |   or peanuts |
| ½ c. water | ½ c. chopped candied cherries |
| ½ tsp. salt | 2 tblsp. butter or margarine |
| 8 c. popped corn | 1 tsp. vanilla |

Combine sugar, corn syrup, water and salt in 2-qt. heavy saucepan. Stir over low heat until sugar is dissolved. Cook over medium heat to hard crack stage (300°).

Meanwhile spread the popcorn, nuts and cherries in a buttered 15½×10½×1″ jelly roll pan and heat in moderate oven (350°) 10 minutes.

Remove syrup from heat; quickly stir in butter and vanilla until butter melts. Pour over popcorn mixture; stir to coat all pieces. Spread thin on flat surface. Cool; then break in pieces. Makes 1¼ pounds.

N O T E : This sweet is not recommended for packing and shipping.

# Cereal Confections

Cereal snacks actually challenge candy in popularity because they so successfully appease the craving for sweets. Another plus: These confections are simple to fix and are relatively inexpensive.

Be sure to try some of our recipes. You'll really brighten a box of Christmas cookies or a plate of candy if you include some Tiny Holiday Wreaths fashioned with corn flakes. Our taste panel voted them among the ten most beautiful and tasty treats made with recipes in this cookbook. The chances are good that you'll agree with this rating.

## TINY HOLIDAY WREATHS

*Candied corn flakes look like holly—you even add red "berries"*

30 marshmallows
½ c. butter (1 stick)
1 tsp. vanilla
2 tsp. green food color

3½ c. corn flakes
Small red candies (for decorating)

Combine marshmallows, butter, vanilla and food color (2 tsp. is correct) in top of double boiler. Heat over water until marshmallows and butter are melted, stirring frequently.

Gradually stir in corn flakes.

Drop from teaspoon onto waxed paper; with hands shape into tiny wreaths, about 1½ to 2″ in diameter. Decorate with small red candies (tiny red hots or other small candies). Makes 33 (2″) wreaths.

N O T E : Instead of tiny wreaths, you can make one big Holiday Wreath (see photo in this book). Drop mixture from spoon in a circle onto waxed paper; with hands, shape to make a 9″ wreath. Decorate with red candied cherries and silver dragées.

## PEANUT CRUNCHIES

*A favorite cereal confection with taste-testers . . . really crunchy*

½ c. dark corn syrup
· ½ c. sugar
¼ tsp. salt

1 c. smooth peanut butter
5 c. corn flakes, lightly crushed

Combine corn syrup, sugar and salt in 1-qt. heavy saucepan. Cook over low heat, stirring constantly until sugar dissolves. Quickly mix in peanut butter and pour over corn flakes, stirring well to mix.

Press into buttered 8″ square pan. Let cool. When almost set, cut in 36 pieces; cool. Makes about 1½ pounds.

## CHILDREN'S PEANUT CHEWS

*Children like to make and eat these*

1 c. dark corn syrup
1 c. sugar
1 c. smooth peanut butter

1¼ c. salted peanuts or dry
    roasted peanuts (6½ oz. can)
5 c. corn flakes

Combine corn syrup and sugar in 3-qt. heavy saucepan. Bring to a full boil, stirring constantly. Remove from heat; quickly stir in peanut butter. Add peanuts and corn flakes, stirring to coat.

Press into buttered 13×9×2″ pan. Cool and cut in 48 pieces. Makes about 2½ pounds.

## CEREAL COOKIE-CANDIES

*Excellent accompaniment to coffee—crisp, peanut-flavored*

1 c. sugar
½ c. light corn syrup
¼ c. butter or margarine
    (½ stick)

¾ c. salted peanuts
5 c. corn flakes

Combine sugar and corn syrup in 2-qt. heavy saucepan. Cook over medium heat, stirring constantly, until sugar dissolves, 2 to 4 minutes. Remove from heat.

Add butter and nuts; stir to distribute butter and to coat nuts. Stir in corn flakes. (A 2-qt. saucepan will be very full, but you can mix in the corn flakes. If you prefer, use a 3-qt. saucepan, but watch cooking sugar and corn syrup very carefully.)

Press into buttered 9″ square pan and cut in 18 pieces, about 2″ each. Makes about 1½ pounds.

NOTE: It's a good idea to warm corn flakes in a moderate oven (350°) 10 minutes before adding them.


## CARAMEL CEREAL CRISPS

*This cereal candy has a marvelous, rich butterscotch taste*

¼ c. butter or margarine
  (½ stick)
1 tblsp. light corn syrup
1 c. dark brown sugar, firmly
  packed

1 tblsp. water
⅛ tsp. salt
3½ c. crisp rice cereal

Combine butter and corn syrup in heavy skillet; place over low heat until butter melts. Add sugar, water and salt. Cook until mixture comes to a full boil, stirring occasionally. Boil 3 minutes or to the firm ball stage (242 to 248°).

Add cereal all at once while still over low heat and stir until evenly coated.

Quickly spread mixture in buttered 13×9×2″ pan. Mark in pieces at once. When cool, turn candy from pan and break in pieces with knife handle. Makes 20 pieces.


## CIRCLE-O CONFECTIONS

*Children like the O's coated with chocolate—let them fix this snack*

1½ c. oat puffs (cereal circles)
1 (6 oz.) pkg. chocolate chips

2 tblsp. shortening
½ c. salted peanuts

Spread cereal in shallow pan and place in very slow oven (250°) about 30 minutes.

Meanwhile, combine chocolate chips and shortening over low heat. Stir in toasted cereal and peanuts.

Drop from teaspoon onto waxed paper. Let stand to set. Makes about 24 confections.

## *Variation*

**Coconut Confections**   Substitute 2 c. flaked coconut for the oat puffs.

## SCOTCH CANDY BARS

*Be sure to warm cereal and nuts to combine with marshmallow*

3 c. oat puffs (cereal circles)
½ c. coarsely chopped salted peanuts
1½ tblsp. butter
1 tblsp. water

2 c. miniature marshmallows
1 tsp. vanilla
½ c. butterscotch-flavored morsels

Combine cereal and nuts in a greased 4- to 5-qt. bowl; place in low oven (150 to 200°) to warm.

Combine butter, water and marshmallows in top of a double boiler; heat, stirring occasionally until marshmallows are melted. Stir in vanilla. Pour at once over warm cereal and nuts, mixing well to combine.

Turn at once into a buttered 9″ square pan and press into an even layer with a buttered spatula. Cool.

Meanwhile, melt butterscotch morsels in small pan over low heat. Cut cooled candy in half lengthwise, making 2 layers. Spread one half with the butterscotch; place other half on top with cut edges together. Cut at once in squares. Makes about 30 pieces, or 1 pound.


## CHOCOLATE CEREAL LOAF

*Dark chocolate contrasts with cereal circles in this chewy confection*

2 c. oat puffs (cereal circles)
1 c. crisp rice cereal
¾ c. chopped walnuts
¾ c. light corn syrup

¼ c. sugar
⅛ tsp. salt
½ tsp. vanilla
1 (6 oz.) pkg. chocolate chips

Combine cereals and nuts in large bowl.

Bring corn syrup and sugar to a full rolling boil in 1-qt. heavy saucepan, stirring constantly.

Remove from heat; add salt, vanilla and chocolate chips; stir until chocolate is melted.

Pour over cereals and nuts and stir until they are coated with syrup. Pack in a 1-qt. paper milk carton, first cutting off top. (Carton should be about 7¼″ tall.)

Chill at least 1 to 2 hours. To serve, loosen loaf with spatula, slip out loaf and cut in thin slices. Makes about 16 slices, 1½ pounds.

## COCOA/PEANUT LOGS

*Children love to make and eat these*

1 (6 oz.) pkg. chocolate chips      4 c. chocolate flavor corn puffs
⅓ c. crunchy peanut butter        (cereal)

Combine chocolate and peanut butter in a 2- to 3-qt. heavy saucepan over medium-low heat. Stir constantly with a wooden spoon until well blended. Add chocolate puffs, stirring over heat only until they are coated with chocolate mixture.

Press firmly into a buttered 9″ square pan. Let stand in a cool place until chocolate is firm. Cut in logs about 3×¾″. Makes about 30 logs, or ¾ pound.

## *Variations*

**Cereal Rocky Road**   Use only 3 c. chocolate cereal, and add 1 c. miniature marshmallows.

**Peanut Logs**   Use 3 to 3½ c. chocolate cereal and add ½ to 1 c. small redskin peanuts.

## SURPRISE CONFECTION BALLS

*Popcorn with surprise ingredients*

28 light caramels (½ lb.)      1 c. salted peanuts
2 tblsp. water               2 c. popped corn
5 c. assorted bite-size, ready-to-    ½ tsp. salt
    serve cereals

Combine caramels with water in saucepan and melt over low heat, stirring.

Combine cereals, peanuts, popped corn and salt in large pan. Pour on hot caramel mixture. Toss with 2 forks to distribute caramel mixture.

Press firmly into 2″ balls, dipping hands in cold water. (Be sure to distribute peanuts.) Makes about 18 balls.

## BUTTERSCOTCH CEREAL TOSS

*Snack is crunchy—butterscotch coating provides rich flavor*

2 qts. assorted bite-size, ready-
to-serve cereals
1 c. salted peanuts
2 c. pretzel sticks
½ c. butter

1½ c. brown sugar
¼ c. dark corn syrup
½ tsp. salt
¼ tsp. ground nutmeg
1 tsp. vanilla

Combine cereals, peanuts and pretzel sticks in large pan or bowl.

Combine butter, brown sugar, corn syrup, salt and nutmeg in saucepan. Bring to a boil; boil 2 minutes. Remove from heat; add vanilla. Pour over cereal mixture; stir to coat all ingredients.

Spread on 2 buttered baking sheets. Let cool until firm. To hasten cooling, place in refrigerator. When set, break in pieces. Makes about 3 quarts.

## BUTTERSCOTCH HAYSTACKS

*Crisp and sweet and so easy to make*

2 (6 oz.) pkgs. butterscotch-
flavored morsels
1½ c. salted cashew nuts

1 (5 oz.) can chow mein
noodles

Melt butterscotch bits in top of double boiler, stirring occasionally to blend.

Meanwhile, combine nuts and chow mein noodles; place in pre-heated low oven (200°). Add warmed nuts and noodles to melted butterscotch and stir until all are coated.

Quickly drop with a dessert spoon onto waxed paper-lined baking sheet to form little haystacks. If nuts and noodles are warmed, butterscotch will not set until all the stacks are spooned out. Makes 48 haystacks, or about 1 pound.

N O T E : You can substitute 1½ c. salted peanuts for the cashews, if you wish.

## CHOCOLATE-TOPPED OAT WAFERS

*Dainty, see-through wafers are crisp, lacy and full of fine flavors*

½ c. butter or margarine
  (1 stick)
¾ c. sugar
½ tsp. ground cinnamon
1 c. quick-cooking rolled oats

2 tblsp. flour
½ tsp. baking powder
1 egg
1 (6 oz.) pkg. chocolate chips

Melt butter in 2-qt. heavy saucepan. Remove from heat. Stir in remaining ingredients, except chocolate. Mix until well blended.

Grease baking sheets and dust lightly with flour. Drop batter in very small amounts from teaspoon 1″ apart onto baking sheets.

Bake in moderate oven (375°) 4 or 5 minutes, or until golden brown. Let stand a minute before removing from baking sheets with sharp, flexible knife. Cool on racks.

Melt chocolate chips over hot water. Frost the smooth underside of wafers, using a small spatula to spread chocolate; then draw the tines of a fork over chocolate to make a design. Cool. Makes 75 thin wafers.

N O T E : If chocolate gets too thick to spread, set saucepan containing it over hot water to warm.

# Bread, Cracker and Cookie

When you want to fix confections that please, reach into the breadbox, or open a box of store cookies, graham or soda crackers. With these modest foods you can create some of today's best confections. The recipes in this section show how to do it.

These confections have many charms. They make exceptionally good eating. They are fast to fix. And they are kind to the pocketbook. That's about all you have a right to expect of any snacks.

## HOLIDAY MERINGUE SQUARES

*Almonds and cherries make this a holiday special*

| | |
|---|---|
| ¼ c. butter | 1 tsp. vanilla |
| 1 c. blanched almonds (or other nuts) | 1 c. sugar |
| | ½ c. crushed soda crackers |
| 2 egg whites | 1 (6 oz.) pkg. chocolate chips |
| ¼ tsp. cream of tartar | or milk chocolate chips (1 c.) |
| ½ tsp. salt | 1 c. halved candied cherries |

Heat butter and almonds in small saucepan; cool to room temperature.

Beat egg whites, cream of tartar, salt and vanilla until foamy. Gradually add sugar, beating until mixture is stiff.

Fold in crackers, chocolate chips and cherries. (Wipe cherries with paper toweling to remove traces of syrup.) Carefully fold in nuts. Spread in a well-buttered 13×9×2″ pan.

Bake in moderate oven (350°) 30 to 35 minutes, or until golden brown. While warm, cut into bars or squares of desired size. Makes 24 (about 2″) squares.

## Variation

**Cherry/Nut Meringues** Omit chocolate pieces from Holiday Meringue Squares; bake and cut in the same way.

## NUT MERINGUE SQUARES

*Take your pick of baked meringue cut in squares or broken in pieces*

| | |
|---|---|
| 2½ c. mixed salted nuts (13 oz.) | ¼ tsp. salt |
| | 1 tsp. vanilla |
| ¼ c. melted butter | 1 c. sugar |
| 2 egg whites | ½ c. crushed soda crackers |
| ¼ tsp. cream of tartar | |

Combine nuts and butter.

Beat egg whites, cream of tartar, salt and vanilla until foamy. Add sugar gradually, continuing to beat until meringue is stiff.

Fold in crushed crackers (crumbs) and then carefully fold in nuts. Spread into well-buttered 13×9×2" pan.

Bake in moderate oven (350°) 30 to 35 minutes, or until golden brown. Cut in squares (about 2") while warm. Cool. Makes 24 squares.

## Variation

**Nut Meringue Flakes** Let Nut Meringue cool without cutting in squares. Then break in pieces.

## MYSTERY DROPS

*Crackers are mystery ingredient. Candy is easy to make, really good*

| | |
|---|---|
| 2 c. sugar | ½ c. finely chopped pecans |
| ⅔ c. milk | 1 tsp. vanilla |
| ¾ c. finely ground soda cracker crumbs (30 crackers) | 7 tblsp. smooth or crunchy peanut butter |

Combine sugar and milk in 2-qt. heavy saucepan. Bring to a boil, stirring until sugar is dissolved. Boil 3 minutes. Remove from heat.

Add remaining ingredients, mixing quickly. Beat until mixture is thick enough to drop from teaspoon onto waxed paper. Makes 33 drops, or about 1½ pounds.

## MOCK ALMOND CRUNCH

*Baked confection made with graham crackers—tastes like toffee*

9 graham crackers
⅓ c. sliced almonds
½ c. brown sugar
½ c. butter

⅛ tsp. almond extract
⅓ c. milk chocolate chips or chocolate chips

Arrange graham cracker squares on bottom of buttered 9" square pan. Sprinkle with almond slices.

Combine brown sugar and butter in small saucepan. Boil 3 minutes. Remove from heat and add almond extract. Pour over graham crackers.

Bake in slow oven (325°) 10 minutes. Remove from oven.

When mixture stops bubbling, sprinkle with chocolate chips. Let stand 10 minutes. Then spread chocolate to frost. Cut in 1½" squares while warm. Makes 36.

## TURTLE SHELLS

*Children love to mold turtles from crumb-coated chocolate mixture*

1½ c. sugar
1 (6 oz.) can evaporated milk (⅔ c.)
2 squares unsweetened chocolate

1 (6¼ oz.) pkg. miniature marshmallows
½ c. chopped pecans
1 c. graham cracker crumbs
1 tsp. vanilla

Combine sugar, evaporated milk and chocolate in 1-qt. heavy saucepan. Bring to a full rolling boil, stirring constantly until sugar dissolves and chocolate blends into mixture. Set aside to cool.

Combine marshmallows and nuts in a big bowl; mix well.

Put cracker crumbs in a shallow pan.

When chocolate mixture is cool, but not cold, add vanilla. Pour over marshmallows and nuts and stir carefully. Drop by spoonfuls onto cracker crumbs. Roll each spoonful of candy to coat with crumbs, then shape like a turtle shell. Place on waxed paper to set, 30 minutes or longer. Makes about 1½ pounds.

## NAPOLEON CREMES

*Creamy layered confections to cut in little pieces—they're rich!*

½ c. butter (1 stick)
¼ c. sugar
¼ c. cocoa
1 tsp. vanilla
1 egg, slightly beaten
2 c. graham cracker crumbs
1 c. flake coconut
½ c. butter (1 stick)

3 tblsp. milk
1 (3¾ oz.) vanilla instant
   pudding mix
2 c. sifted confectioners sugar
1 (6 oz.) pkg. chocolate chips
2 tblsp. butter
1 tblsp. paraffin (optional)

Combine ½ c. butter, sugar, cocoa and vanilla in top of double boiler. Cook over simmering water until butter melts. Stir in egg. Continue cooking, stirring, until mixture is thick, about 3 minutes. Blend in crumbs and coconut. Press into buttered 9″ square pan.

Cream ½ c. butter thoroughly. Stir in milk, pudding mix and confectioners sugar. Beat until light and fluffy. Spread evenly over crust. Chill until firm.

Melt chocolate, 2 tblsp. butter and paraffin over simmering water. Cool. Spread over pudding layer. Chill. Cut in 2×¾″ bars. Makes about 44 pieces.

## FROZEN CHOCOLATE CUPS

*This frozen chocolate confection is finger food. It makes a delightful small dessert to serve at a buffet supper*

1 c. butter (2 sticks)
2 c. confectioners sugar
4 squares unsweetened chocolate,
   melted
4 eggs, beaten

1 tsp. rum or peppermint extract
1 tsp. vanilla
1½ c. vanilla wafer crumbs
36 small paper baking cups
   (about 1¼″ across bottom)

Place butter in large bowl of electric mixer and allow to stand at room temperature until soft. Add confectioners sugar, and cream together by hand. Add chocolate, eggs and flavorings; beat with electric mixer until thoroughly combined and fluffy, 2 to 3 minutes.

Place 1 tsp. vanilla wafer crumbs in bottom of each paper cup. Set each in a paper nut cup of similar size to reinforce cup that holds confection. Or set in smallest size muffin-pan cups, if you have them.

With a pointed teaspoon (not rounded measuring spoon), fill two thirds full of chocolate mixture, rounding top slightly. Sprinkle top of each with additional 1 tsp. crumbs.

Place on trays and put in freezer. When frozen solid, remove candy cups from supporting nut cups or muffin-pan cups. Package them in a box with waxed paper between layers, wrap in aluminum foil and put in freezer. Or put in plastic bags; close tightly and freeze (they keep indefinitely in freezer).

When ready to use, remove from freezer and serve in the cups. Makes 36 confections.

## ORANGE/CHOCOLATE BALLS

*Taste-testers really liked these*

3 c. vanilla wafer crumbs
  (12 oz. pkg.)
1 c. sifted confectioners sugar
¼ c. cocoa
1½ c. finely chopped or
  ground walnuts

¼ c. light or dark corn syrup
½ c. frozen orange juice
  concentrate

Combine all ingredients in a 2-qt. mixing bowl. Mix and knead with hands to form solid masses, adding a little more corn syrup if necessary to make ingredients stick together.

Roll mixture into balls ¾ to 1" in size. Store in airtight container in refrigerator and let stand a few days before serving; flavor improves on ripening. Makes 50 to 60 pieces, or 2 pounds.

NOTE: You can give the balls a frosted look by rolling them in confectioners sugar.

## CHOCOLATE-COATED CRISPIES

*You dip toasted bread in chocolate and come up with a great treat!*

6 slices bread
1 tblsp. melted butter

1 (6 oz.) pkg. chocolate chips
2 tblsp. shortening

Trim crusts from bread. Butter slices lightly. Cut in 1" squares. Toast in very slow oven (250°) 1 hour, turning every 15 minutes.

Melt chocolate chips with shortening in saucepan over low heat. Stir until smooth. Remove from heat.

With 2 forks, dip squares of bread in chocolate to coat. Place on wire rack to permit chocolate to set. Makes about 8 dozen squares.

## Variation

**Chocolate-Coated Crackerettes** Spread 2 c. oyster crackers in shallow pan. Brush lightly with butter. Toast and dip in chocolate like bread squares.

## SKILLET CARAMEL CRISPIES

*Confection starts out as bread . . . serve it with fruit juice or tea*

| | |
|---|---|
| ½ c. brown sugar | 24 (2″) bread squares (day old |
| ½ c. butter | bread) |
| ¼ c. finely chopped nuts (optional) | |

Melt brown sugar and butter together in small saucepan. Boil 2 minutes. Add nuts. Remove from heat.

Dip bread squares in hot brown sugar mixture and fry in buttered skillet over medium heat until golden and caramel-like on both sides. Turn every 2 or 3 minutes while browning. Total time for pan-frying is 8 to 10 minutes. (You can dip more squares in caramel that melts off into skillet during cooking.) Cool on racks. Makes 24.

## Variation

**Coconut Caramel Crispies** Substitute ¼ c. flaked coconut for the nuts.

# Index